SERIES TITLE PAGE

This Ministry of Helps manual is the first in a series of three works intended as a resource for pastors and church leaders eager to get more people involved in the work of the ministry in their local bodies. This is a reference manual you can use as a model for creating your local church ministries manual.

The second is the presenter's manual for *The 12-Week Ministry of Helps Training Program*. It is an addendum to this manual and can be used to teach Ministry of Helps classes at your local congregation. This addendum can be used repeatedly for successive training classes.

The third work is *Adventures in Service to God*, a workbook, which goes along with the presenter's manual. It is available in downloadable format for smartphones, e-readers, and tablets and is available in book form wherever books are sold.

Each participant should have a physical copy so he or she can make notations in the text or on electronic devices to refer to in class. If participants are using e-books, they should also have pen and paper to take notes on matters the local church has to change to comply with pastoral or denominational preferences.

A Resource for Charismatic and Pentecostal Congregations

The Ministry of Helps

A Manual for Local Church Organization

Rev. Lawrence C. Spencer

WESTBOW
PRESS®
A DIVISION OF THOMAS NELSON
& ZONDERVAN

WestBow Press books may be ordered through booksellers or by contacting:

WestBow Press
A Division of Thomas Nelson & Zondervan
1663 Liberty Drive
Bloomington, IN 47403
www.westbowpress.com
1 (866) 928-1240

ISBN: 978-1-5127-7276-0 (sc)
ISBN: 978-1-5127-7277-7 (e)

Library of Congress Control Number: 2017900897

Print information available on the last page.

WestBow Press rev. date: 2/9/2017

CONTENTS

Appendix I to The Ministries of Helps Manual

DEDICATION

I dedicate this manual to Ladonna Spencer, my wife, who has encouraged me and helped me choose words and scriptures in this manual. Without her help, it would never have come to fruition.

I dedicate it as well to the hundreds of students who have gone through the training and have given me feedback that has made this final copy better than if I had done it myself.

FOREWORD

This manual is offered as a planning tool to pastors, directors of support ministries, and others interested in working in God's service in local churches.

I stress at the outset that work in a church is not a substitute for faith, for a prayer life, or for closeness to God. Working hard for God should be the result of these commitments to Him.

Successful people in the Ministry of Helps are examples of folks living the life God intends for them. They walk in love, divine health, and prosperity and praise God at all times. Also, they never neglect family to work in the church. This includes pastors; we have a Helps Ministry to take the burden off pastors! Never do you hear a bad confession out of responsible Helps workers; never do they criticize their pastors or lead dissenters in a church.

This is not to suggest that Helps workers are perfect; they just set examples for Helps workers to follow. As the chapters unfold, further guidance and suggestions are offered.

Purchasers of this manual are authorized by the copyright owner to duplicate forms for their local churches only. However, no charge can be made nor can the manual or any training program be duplicated for sale without express written permission of the copyright owner or WestBow Press. All other rights reserved.

PREFACE

Over the past thirty years, we have noticed the Holy Spirit move a lot more easily and frequently in churches that organized out the chaos.

Pastors have a hard enough job allocating their time to minister to their flocks and take time for family, so doing the more mundane tasks in the church is not given as high a priority. Forward-thinking pastors delegate these non-spiritual tasks to volunteers in their congregation. We use Jesus for our example when He fed the multitudes. He took care of the miracle, and the workers distributed the loaves and fishes.

The best-case scenario is found in a church, big or small, in which everything is tidy; ushers, other greeters, and helpers make guests welcome; follow-up occurs during the week to thank guests; and the parking is easy and the lots are clean. Visitors here are comfortable and can listen and receive God's Word without being distracted.

Conversely, some congregations have facilities that are not well maintained, untidy parking lots or exteriors, poor lighting inside or outside, heating or air conditioning set wrong, and music poorly planned or played. They can also have disorganized church workers, poor financial stewardship, and other evidence of disorganization. Any combination of these things can take people's attention off the preaching of the Word.

And other congregations are not growing; these are places where the Holy Spirit does not often move. A church God has not sent new people to is perhaps a church incapable of ministering to more people.

I have had elders argue that I was trying to organize the Holy Spirit out of our service or that theirs was not a liturgical church and didn't have to do things the same way every time. On the contrary, if you organize the non-spiritual parts of your church, the spiritual part, which is led by the Holy Spirit, can move more freely.

People may not compliment you on your clean restrooms, but untidy restrooms will cause many to never come back. Also, if parking is difficult or inconvenient, people simply will not come. If you are having chronic money challenges, people will have legitimate reasons for questioning the congregation's faithfulness to the tithe and the church's financial management.

Read the manual, glean what can to improve your church, and don't try to fix something if it isn't broken. If you don't do one or more tasks the way this manual suggests because your way is working fine, why change? Just set in writing the manner of doing all jobs in your church and make sure all involved get copies of your best practices.

God bless you and your efforts in leading your congregation.

—LS

ACKNOWLEDGMENTS

I want to thank a number of people for assisting me in collecting information and writing this manual.

About thirty years ago, I attended an usher training class taught by Scott Schaffer of the Jubilee Christian Center in San Jose, California. His presentation inspired me to put in writing a process that helps congregations organize the non-spiritual part of their operations so the spiritual part would be unimpeded by distractions.

A year or so later, Jubilee hosted the Regional School of Helps, which was taught by Dr. Robert Lemon, Dr. Michael Landsman, and Rev. Buddy Bell from Tulsa, Oklahoma. These three gave me the tools and the basic formats to put together the information in a church procedures manual.

My pastor at the time was the late Rev. Ernie Longley of the Word of Life Christian Fellowship in Salinas, California. He asked me to organize a Ministry of Helps in his church and write a training program to teach the workers. That is where the Presenter's and Participant's Manuals were born.

I also thank WestBow Press for giving me the ability to publish the work so it could be distributed.

I hope to encourage and inspire churches to raise up and train the next generation of workers who can assist in getting God's message of salvation out to a lost and dying world.

Thanks,

—LS

Magalia, California

2016

INTRODUCTION

Among the multitude of challenges that face pastors, two come quickly to mind. First, they have a burden of souls and seek to grow their churches to serve new believers. Second, most of them know they do not have enough time to seek God and prepare sermons, the spiritual work of the church, because their time is taken up with trying to accomplish the busy work needed around their churches.

I once had a pastor who was often unprepared for a service because he had been busy helping a parishioner with some chores, or church maintenance, or a myriad other duties needed to keep a church going. The result is that the church stayed the same size. Some leave, others enter, but no growth is apparent despite the talents of the pastor. God is apparently making sure the pastor has only the amount of people he or she can handle.

The ancient church had some of the same challenges we face today.

> Now in those days, when the number of the disciples was multiplying, there arose a complaint against the Hebrews by the Hellenists, because their widows were neglected in the daily distribution. Then the twelve summoned the multitude of the disciples and said, "It is not desirable that we should leave the word of God and serve tables. [Read this as "doing manual labor"] Therefore, brethren, seek out from among you seven men of good reputation, full of the Holy Spirit and wisdom, whom we may appoint over this business (the manual labor); but we will give ourselves continually to prayer and to the ministry of the word. (Acts 6:1–4)

It was even bringing strife to the local body. What did they do? What was the result? The first thing the apostles did was pick people they knew to be wise and had received the baptism of the Holy Spirit. They appointed them to handle practical ministerial duties, the manual labor. This freed the apostles to minister the Word of God. God's way is so simple, and our grandiose plans just waste time and get nothing done. I vote for God's way!

Pastors need to learn from the apostles and delegate this business so they will be free to do the spiritual work that promotes God's church. This manual gives a roadmap for accomplishing the goal of choosing and training people and tips for managing them.

The result of doing it God's way is in Acts 6:7: "Then the word of God spread, and the number of the disciples multiplied greatly in Jerusalem, and a great many of the priests were obedient to the faith."

Let's consider the three things that happened when the apostles took these steps and endeavor to make them happen in our church.

- First, the Word of God increased; more preaching and teaching occurred.
- Second, the church grew in numbers and the disciples multiplied.
- Third, God gave them a bonus. Many Jewish priests became obedient to the faith. Remember that in those days, Christianity was an offshoot of Judaism, not a separate body, so converting a rabbi was a big deal.

The Word gives us instructions on how to free up a pastor's time and how to grow the church in Acts 6:1–7, so let's not reinvent the wheel. God has given us specific instructions in his Instruction Manual, the Bible, so let's take His exhortation to heart and do what He tells us should be done.

The purpose of the Helps Ministry is to further the preaching of the gospel and the winning of new souls by taking duties away from the pulpit and putting them in the hands of the saints. Those in ministerial offices as outlined in Ephesians 4:11 can get on with their appointed tasks. Similarly, those serving in lay ministerial offices as outlined in Romans 12 can do the "work of the ministry."

The spiritual gifts outlined in 1 Corinthians 12 are used by the fivefold ministers in Ephesians 11 and the saints in general to empower all Christians to do the spiritual or practical jobs needed in the church body.

The Bible tells us that the first thing the pastor and the leadership must do is choose Spirit-filled saints to fill jobs in the local church. In the ancient church, this was an easier task because many of the people chosen had been followers of Jesus while He was still in His earthly ministry. We must assume that these people had been observed by the apostles and proven themselves faithful over possibly two or three years of service. For Stephen, Phillip, Procorus, Nicanor, Timon, Parmenas, and Nicholas, this was likely a promotion to a higher level and to formal responsibility. They had been faithful followers or they would have not been on the short list of potential leaders.

The Bible tells us that Stephen quickly became a great man of faith. He did great wonders and miracles and was the first Christian martyr. Philip too rose to the office of evangelist and possibly an apostle. Both of these men are examples of ordinary church members who answered the call of the leadership of the church. When called, they worked diligently at lowly tasks and proved themselves faithful in the judgment of the apostles. They were promoted and were eventually able to do great works for God wherever He placed them.

In the modern church, people move around geographically and leadership does not get to observe them for years as neighbors as they did in biblical times. So we must make up for this lost time and find, train, and evaluate people God has sent our way and appoint our own people known to be full of the Spirit and wisdom. Then, as they did in Acts, we must turn over the responsibility for servanthood to them so the fivefold ministry (prophets, apostles, evangelists, pastors, and teachers) can do the work of preparing the saints to do God's work.

Training and Selecting Workers for the Helps Ministry

We have outlined the need for workers and discovered God's methodology for meeting the needs of the local church. He gave us brains and free wills, so now it is up to us to develop the format for completing His instructions in our churches.

First, let us identify those who have a desire to help. An obvious start is those who feel the call to full-time ministry and students planning to attend Bible school or seminary. In fact, it should be mandatory for these first two groups. Then you have good people who just have a desire to be of service. Those who have been in ministry in other churches can also be attracted back into service. Others might be people with a desire to help with no long-term goal of full-time ministry.

Second, to attract other new workers who have previously not thought of service in the local church, we should advertise! Also, we make it an exclusive group. Only those who have completed the training and evaluation program should be admitted. This will tell the congregation that the workers assisting them are committed, and it will attract those who want to belong to something bigger than self.

Those desiring full-time ministry would not be recommended by the pastor until they had completed Helps training and served satisfactorily as helpers in the local church. This is in keeping with Acts 6:3: "Therefore, brethren, seek out from among you seven men of good reputation, full of the Holy Spirit and wisdom, whom we may appoint over this business."

Following the above, the Bible makes membership exclusive; only those who have accepted Jesus as their personal Savior can be members.

> For with the heart one believes unto righteousness, and with the mouth confession is made unto salvation. For the Scripture says, "Whoever believes on Him will not be put to shame." For there is no distinction between Jew and Greek, for the same Lord over all is rich to all who call upon Him. For "whoever calls on the name of the Lord shall be saved." (Romans 10:10–13)

By adhering to biblical principles, volunteer church work stops being a chore and becomes an honor. In human terms, exclusivity creates desire. There were more than seventy helpers following Jesus, probably more. Why did the apostles choose only seven? We have to be picky too. The Bible shows us that not everyone who aspires to be a church worker will make it.

Finally, we should have a Code of Conduct that includes a time commitment. People want an outline of what is expected and what constitutes a job well done. They also do not want long-term commitments. This is not biblical, but we are dealing with modern people here, some of them not longtime Christians. God commits to an eternity of loving and caring for us; we just haven't gotten that yet. If we can commit 100 percent to God for life, we can bear their not wanting to commit to a local body at first.

There is a sense of belonging, being part of something bigger that comes from a formal commitment and a formal acceptance by someone in authority. A six-month time commitment should be the maximum to start. After six months, the person can leave with no reason given and no explanation asked for. Those who choose to reenlist can do so if their performance has been satisfactory and if they have lived up to the Code of Conduct. Volunteers and leaders alike can end the situation without bad feelings.

Let's formalize training for leaders and those who choose enlist in the Helps Ministry. We can teach them specifics about the Word and fundamentals of the faith. Thus, we as leaders can "know they are full of the Spirit and wisdom" (Acts 6:8), and they can serve in leaderships or workers' positions. We must assure ourselves that we "know" all the workers to be "full of the spirit and wisdom" and secure enough in their Christian walk to be effective witnesses for Him. We can do this only by observation. Standardized training can shorten the time and allow leadership to evaluate workers and more quickly integrate them into worker and then leadership roles. We can observe them during training programs and church activities and make the judgment God tells us to make prior to bringing them into formal service.

Why should people agree to go through a training program if they already are in the ministry? The answer is simple; many of your leaders have learned the basics in Bible school, seminaries, or other churches. They may have years of experiencing traditions, sermons, or other Christian teachings. The positive is that their past training and experience will make leaders more diverse. The negative is that as their new pastor, you do not know what they learned at previous churches or ministries and how it may differ from your methodology.

The leadership of your church must know everyone is teaching the program the same way. Thus, a new believer can hear about salvation from anyone in the Helps Ministry or any leader and the manner of presentation will be similar.

Another very important point is that the leadership has to have experienced the training themselves and perhaps participated in teaching it. They will then be able to later judge others' progress in the program knowing what basic teaching they have received. The graduates of the program are tomorrow's leadership; they will be judging the next group and so on. Everyone must hear the foundational truths in the same format so they cannot only judge the next generation but also help improve the program. Here, pastors can make giant contributions to the success of the endeavor by teaching a portion of each group's instruction.

As leaders complete their classes, they can be rotated to teach some of the classes. The instruction becomes an integral part of the culture of the local church. When everybody in leadership is on the same page, positive things happen.

In the gospels, Jesus addressed points like who was to be the greatest among His helpers. He perceived jealousy and the desire to be the boss in His disciples. The cost of following Him was putting Him before family and possessions and sending out the seventy (or seventy-two). In these passages, He was preparing us for when He would be gone from His earthly ministry. He knew we would have to deal with organizing His church, so He gave us the tools to do that.

Your training program and the organization of the Helps Ministry must follow Jesus's example. All should humble themselves and put Him first—no fiefdoms or cliques in the church. Two by two mentioned in the Bible manifests in a local body and suggests having a backup person who can do the same job so the positions can be rotated. Thus, no one becomes indispensable.

Jesus did not leave His ministry until He had trained many replacements. As a bonus, He left the Holy Spirit to teach us what we should do. Thus, no one in Helps can be promoted until his or her replacement has been trained and is in place. Again, we cannot compromise the Word; if we don't do it God's way, we are just doing church work instead of God's work.

Additionally, many people who are filling worker and leadership roles got those jobs because the slots needed filling and they were willing to help. In many cases, they had special talents, like musical talents, and were available. Usually, no one formally examined their knowledge of what being a Christian worker was all about. At times, people were appointed to leadership positions but hadn't been baptized in the Holy Spirit! If a new baby Christian asked them for any instruction about baptism in the Holy Spirit, they would not have a clue about what to do or say. It is imperative that all workers be capable witnesses of the gifts of the Spirit.

Many Christian workers cannot clearly and comfortably explain salvation, healing, baptism in the Holy Spirit, or deliverance at least not in simple, easy-to-understand terms. Pastors have a vested interest in making sure that all workers can lead others to an understanding of Christianity's basics. The challenge is clarity and comfort, and that can happen only after formal training and a demonstration of that ability to the pastor.

What Should the Training Include?

Again, we look to the Bible. Acts 6 showed us how to choose; Jesus said, "Feed my sheep." He told us to win souls. He said that we would do greater works in His name than He had done. This is hard for some to figure out after over 2,000 years. So the program must explain clearly how to get people saved and be baptized in the Holy Spirit and how deliverance, healing, and other miracles are still valid today.

It should also include a history of the denomination and of the local church—how our denomination and other denominations are governed. Who does what and why? Faithfulness and commitment as demonstrated by biblical characters and how that applies today.

- the biblical teachings on the various gifts
- ministerial gifts in Ephesians 4
- the Holy Spirit's gifts in 1 Corinthians 12
- the motivational gifts in Romans 12

Every Christian should know them and the differences between the various gifts and be able to explain them.

The appendix to this manual contains a training program that can be used as is or modified a bit to conform to local traditions and denominational preferences.

Selling the Concept to a Congregation

Why should we even think about having to "sell" our members on serving? In answer, let us look at Moses's ministry. He promised freedom and a homeland to millions if they followed him. God provided many miracles to convince them that Moses was the "man," and that solidified his claim to leadership from God. When Moses led them out, their former oppressors gave them riches, food was provided every day by God, and their shoes did not wear out. Despite all this, Moses still had a problem keeping them committed, so we should not be surprised that it is difficult to get volunteers and we experience a lack of commitment today.

If we think people today are any different from the Jews of Moses's time, we are mistaken. We have more miracles to point to than the ancient Jews ever thought of. We have the Messiah they only dreamed of, and we still fight the commitment battle. We have it too easy today. Faith is not perceived as needed for daily survival. Most go to God only when things are tough instead of praising Him daily for all His blessings, so we have the same challenge Moses had. Also, remember how the apostles and followers of Jesus fled after His arrest. People can lose faith and interest quickly in some circumstances.

How do you build faith? "So then faith comes by hearing, and hearing by the word of God" (Romans 10:17). Clearly in modern understanding, it is listening to and really understanding God's Word. Our training program must be biblically based and stress using the Bible as the primary source for answers. The pastor introduces the concept using Jesus's admonition in Luke 10:2 that there is a lot of work to do and not enough people to do it! "And the things that you have heard from me among many witnesses, commit these to faithful men who will be able to teach others also" (2 Timothy 2:2).

Remember the Great Commission: "Go and make disciples of all nations." He directed us to not only get people saved but to make disciples of them, to train them and bring them into the fullness of the faith. So building excitement of something to come is very important via perhaps a series of sermons or announcements or overhead projections suggesting something big is coming—a deliberate and well-planned movement to encourage members to volunteer.

Let us make entry a formal rite of passage. Jesus did that when He sent out the seventy, and the apostles did it when they appointed the seven. Hands were laid on them, and the apostles anointed them with oil. Thus, after a period of testing and training, a ceremony of sorts was held that added them or sent them out. There was in ancient times and should be in our time a time where the church member is formally inducted into the group as a Helps minister.

Make it exclusive. Applications should be taken for a set time; all existing workers must put in applications too. The pastor and leadership will review and pray over the applications and choose the members of the first class. Some leaders should be in the first class because they will be teaching later and need to experience the program firsthand; if not in the first series, then it should be for sure in later classes. Again, this gets everyone on the same page and sends a message to the congregation that all the leadership has gone through the training and now the leaders are teaching it. No one is greater or lesser.

In churches in which the Helps Ministry is highly organized, as was the case with the feeding of the 5,000, great ministry happens. Jesus's preaching was not interrupted by the manual task of passing out food; it was done quickly and quietly by scores of ordinary "ushers" who participated in a fantastic miracle. That is the measure by which we can judge our work; workers today can do the same. By committing to helping God's work in a local church, they too can be participants in salvations, baptisms in the Holy Spirit, and all sorts of miracles. Participants? Wow!

The Process of Developing a Helps Ministry

The chronology usually looks like this.

1. The pastor decides to form a Helps Ministry to assist in running the church.

2. The pastor solicits input from the council or elders; if the leadership is not in agreement, the congregation probably won't be either. This is the principle of the "multitude of counsel."

3. A series of announcements let the congregation know what is coming up and why it is important to the church. This is the "sale."

4. A Code of Conduct is developed for only the workers, not the people in the congregation; that should be made very clear.

5. The presenter's manual (appendix 1 in this manual) is used to teach the class. Pastors are encouraged to teach as many of these classes as possible to get to know the workers.

6. The first year, the class should probably be held three times, thirty-six out of fifty-two weeks, another reason why leaders must either be trained separately or graduate with the first group and be able to share the teaching burden.

7. The second year, the class might be held only twice—it becomes more exclusive and harder to qualify. A person who wants to serve has to go through the process over a long period during which time he or she is observed and judged "wise and full of the Holy Spirit" (Acts 6).

8. The church should purchase sufficient participants' workbooks for all planned classes and sell them to the participants to recoup the cost. If you give the manuals for free, attendees will not appreciate them as much as if they had to pay for them themselves.

9. Participants have to complete all twelve classes to graduate. They must agree to the Code of Conduct and agree to a six-month time commitment.

10. At the end of the twelve weeks, the graduates are anointed with oil during a ceremony held at the church and presented with a church-specific certificate.

11. Makeup dates should be scheduled as needed for those who miss a class. A one-year grace period for existing church workers should start from the date of the first class. At the end of the year, only those current workers who have completed the program can participate as helpers or in leadership positions.

12. Those who do not finish will need to take a vacation from service until the classes are made up; this will prevent others from becoming resentful.

13. The attendance policy emphasizes the exclusivity of membership in ministry and the level of commitment required. Those who cannot commit will be welcomed and loved as parishioners but not receive formal jobs or church responsibilities.

Why Twelve Weeks?

First of all, it's to see who will commit to attend and submit to leadership; many will commit to a single or a couple of meetings, but if they can last twelve weeks, that's a better indication of serious interest and commitment to the program.

Second, this affords the pastors and elders (two or three must attend every session) to get to know the participants—what they say and how they live out their Christian walks. This fulfills the scriptural admonition to choose workers whom you know are biblically qualified to be in ministry; Acts 6:3: "Therefore, brethren, seek out from among you seven men of good reputation, full of the Holy Spirit and wisdom, whom we may appoint over this business."

Third, it gives the new workers the chance to "Know who labors among you."

> And we urge you, brethren, to recognize those who labor among you, and are
> over you in the Lord and admonish you, and to esteem them very highly in love
> for their work's sake. Be at peace among yourselves. (1 Thessalonians 5:12–13)

In a larger church, this may be the only time the person gets to interact with the pastor personally.

This manual contains outlines of the many ministries a church might like to create. It contains a chapter on how to make a ministry outline for those who want to create one not listed. It is a helpful tool for a pastor or leader who has not been able to put a formal organization in place. Chapters can be revised, rewritten, and tailored for your congregation. If you follow the formatting in this manual for all your ministries, the rules and organization of all ministries will be similar in format.

An organizational plan and an organizational chart should be created and posted in the church. All members and guests should be able to see the various functions of the church and who reports to whom. Maintaining a chain of command eliminates the need and the burden of having everyone report to the pastor.

The first question the pastor should ask when a worker complains about a situation is, "What did your supervisor say when you mentioned it to him or her?" Pastors cannot expect a Helps Ministry to survive if they overrule their appointed ministry leaders.

Jobs should be rotated periodically. Everyone should be able to participate as an usher and an exhorter of the Word. Short stints at another job or discipline trains backups and prevents cliques from developing.

Limit the number of people who report to the pastor. This is difficult because everyone wants a "piece" of the pastor, and as the disciples discussed, who is the greater? (Luke 22:24). People desire to be the confidant of the pastor, but as the congregation grows, it will be impossible for everyone to report directly to the pastor. Pastors may resist this as diluting their authority, but it is essential to success. See Genesis 18:21, when Moses's father-in-law admonished him to get some help!

Pastors of other affiliated or denominational churches can be given this outline and invited to send their Helps leadership. We can train them and send them out and increase the impact our Helps Ministry has on saints we may never meet.

This introduction can be the structure for announcements, sermons, discussions with leadership, and background knowledge of the necessity of a Helps Ministry.

CHAPTER 1

General Qualifications for Participation in the Helps Ministry

The Bible is our guide for choosing, training, and evaluating all those who aspire to ministry in the church. Let our guide be 1 Timothy 3:1–7.

> This is a faithful saying: If a man desires the position of a bishop, he desires a good work. A bishop then must be blameless, the husband of one wife, temperate, sober-minded, of good behavior, hospitable, able to teach; not given to wine, not violent, not greedy for money, but gentle, not quarrelsome, not covetous; one who rules his own house well, having his children in submission with all reverence (for if a man does not know how to rule his own house, how will he take care of the church of God?); not a novice, lest being puffed up with pride he fall into the same condemnation as the devil. Moreover he must have a good testimony among those who are outside, lest he fall into reproach and the snare of the devil.

These verses describe the characteristics of those we consider today to be staff or those in the fivefold ministry gifts of Ephesians 4:11. Verses 8–14 speak to the folks whom this manual is more concerned with. Deacons, or *diakonoi* in Greek, is a term used for workers, servants, or subordinate officials waiting on and assisting higher officials. In our case, it is local church workers assisting the pastor in doing God's work.

Continuing in 1 Timothy 3:8–13,

> Likewise deacons must be reverent, not double-tongued, not given to much wine, not greedy for money, holding the mystery of the faith with a pure conscience. But let these also first be tested; then let them serve as deacons, being found blameless. Likewise, their wives must be reverent, not slanderers, temperate, faithful in all things. Let deacons be the husbands of one wife, ruling their children and their own houses well. For those who have served well as deacons obtain for themselves a good standing and great boldness in the faith which is in Christ Jesus.

We need to understand that training church workers is a biblical standard, not something locally created to control people. Not just anyone who comes in the door aspiring to minister in our churches will be placed in ministry. The Bible is clear that we need to select and know those who labor among us. To that end, this manual is intended to assist pastors and those in leadership to train, equip, and evaluate those who work in any capacity in the church.

We believe that people should aspire to positions of trust in the church as opposed to being drafted into them by others. If people perceive that working in the church is a burden, that they are being used, or that they are not appreciated or recognized, you will soon lose them.

Setting up standards to qualify to work is a win-win for everyone. The congregation will know that the workers have had to do something to qualify to become workers, and the workers will perceive that they had to do something extra—not just be available, willing laborers.

We believe that working in God's service is an honor and a privilege to be coveted by those who work in the church; they should consider serving not a burden but a joy. To accomplish that, we must be mindful that perfection is not demanded—only the diligent pursuit of growth in the Christian lives of the workers. By setting standards, the workers know what is expected of them and what a good job looks like. Leadership can hold them accountable for the proper performance of their tasks, and the workers can feel secure that the leadership cares enough to scrutinize their work and recognize jobs well done.

Having job descriptions helps everyone know who is responsible for what. It promotes efficiency and smooth operation of the routine tasks of the church. By doing so, the pastor and other ministers are not constantly having to take time from ministry to sort out who does what. Everyone will have a leader, and everyone will know his or her job and be trained to do it. Accountability up and down and to God will be present in every endeavor. Wherever the Bible is specific on how something is to be done, that will be the way it is done. Where the Bible gives latitude, leadership will decide how things are to be done. Discussions about how things are done shall be confined to training and other meetings, never during a service.

We will have a Code of Conduct. Workers and the congregation must understand that this Code of Conduct is for the ministers and workers only. The general congregation will not have to abide by those rules (except voluntarily should they want to join the Helps Ministry). Conduct that would preclude a congregation member from being a worker will absolutely not prevent him or her from attending the church.

Qualifications and Recordkeeping

Acts 6:3 mentions they should be "full of the Holy Spirit and wise." Availability is more important than ability, and willing people bring joy to the job. A happy crew will attract new workers and help get new converts too. The workers exemplify the Christian life to the babes! Studying the Word of God transforms their minds (Romans 12:2; 2 Timothy 2:15). They should speak with one accord; no strife or backbiting (1 Corinthians 1:10; Mark 9:33–39, 43–50).

Potential workers should submit written applications outlining their chosen fields of service. The leadership then knows the desires of the applicants and can put them in jobs they want or are qualified for. They should agree in writing to abide by the Code of Conduct.

Keep accurate records of all training classes, use sign-in sheets, and keep the records permanently. Signed codes of conduct and the listings of training schools attended should be in a file for each worker.

The Helps Ministry was given by God to the church in 1 Corinthians 12:28. We represent Him to the people we minister to. Everyone aspiring to the Helps Ministry should take this responsibility seriously. Members' applications, their prayerful consideration of leadership, and subsequent training lead to their entry into the Ministry of Helps.

As a Helps Ministry worker, you will be asked to read, sign, and agree to abide by the Code of Conduct. Some of the provisions may be a challenge to you, and some may be of no concern because you live that way now. However, we expect you to live up to all of them. If you feel that the standards are too restrictive, please discuss it in private with the pastor or Helps Ministry leader before you apply.

If you apply and are accepted but then fail to live up to the standards, that places you and the leadership in the potentially uncomfortable position of having to discuss your conduct and perhaps ask for your resignation. That is a waste of your time and very sad for all concerned.

At the end of this chapter is a suggested Code of Conduct. Use it or modify it as your church deems appropriate. What is important is simply that you have one. People feel more secure if they know what is expected of them. Leadership will find it easier to be fair and evenhanded in evaluating the conduct of those entrusted to them.

From time to time, someone may fall short in one or more of the standards. Resist the temptation to fill a needed position with someone who has not or will not adhere to the standards everyone else has to. It will destroy morale, and your integrity will be questioned. Also, it could cause someone else to stray by following the bad example of a supposedly qualified Helps Ministry worker.

Consider Proverbs 29:2: "When the righteous are in authority, the people rejoice; But when a wicked man rules, the people groan." This explains what most of us have learned in our secular jobs. When good people are running the operation, people are happy to help. However, when inept or the wrong people are in charge of things, workers are invariably not happy. In a church setting, where the workers are not depending on a paycheck, they will leave. Sometimes, this can be right in the middle of a job, and often, they can just leave your church altogether. Pastors must choose their leaders wisely.

Concerning the entire training program, be inspired by Proverbs 4:13, 9:9, and 15:9. These are just a few of many scriptures you can quote when individuals feel they don't have to attend the classes because they have been in ministry for so many years and already know how to do their jobs. That's not the point; by attending and supporting the training program, the veterans help set the example of submission to the new program. The new recruits will feel that it really is worth taking the time if the old hands have to do it as well.

This has been a problem. Many churches have had current workers who absolutely refuse to go through the program and have dozens of excuses. If you grant exceptions, you will regret that. I have seen it done, and people have paid the price. There can be dissention, claims of favoritism, and feelings of superiority by the one granted the exception. This caused problems in recruiting and in future disciplining when necessary of the one granted the exception. It is fraught with danger.

The Bible is clear that we have to have standards and that we are not to compromise them and let "wicked" people in ministry. In the Hebrew, the word *wicked* is *rawshaw*—a person who is morally wrong or an "actively bad" person. Those who deliberately and defiantly do not live up to the code can be considered actively bad insofar as their agreement and adherence to the code. They may not be bad folk, but they are defying local leadership. For example, those who cannot or will not keep their kids under control would not be classed as "bad" people, but they would not be qualified to serve because by choice they have decided not to discipline their kids to behave in church. They have made their choice; the leadership has to stand firm and refrain from appointing them as workers. You can take many of the topics in the code and construct examples in which a person is not bad but is not someone we want in our Helps Ministry.

Pastors and other ministers should feel free to change this code or any other part of this manual to fit their denominational customs and doctrine. As previously mentioned, at the end of this chapter are a format for a Helps Worker Application and a copy of the suggested Code of Conduct.

As a member of the Helps Ministry I agree to this Code of conduct;

1. To speak in one accord with the leadership of this church. 1 Cor. 1:10 Any differences of opinion are to be discussed in Helps Ministry Training classes like this one, or privately with the person involved. Matt. 18:15-17

2. To Live a Clean Life. 1 Cor. 6:19-20 I will not defile the Temple of God (my body) with smoking, drinking alcoholic beverages, using illicit drugs, immoral sex, or other unhealthy practices1 Tim 3:2.

3. As an example of self-control and respectability, I will keep myself clean of body and breath, and dress in clean and appropriate clothes as a living example of how Jesus would have me look as His representative on earth

4. In the spirit of Matt. 24:45-46. I will faithfully be on time to and attend all church services when I am scheduled to work. I will never miss a function where I am scheduled to work without getting a substitute. (Emergencies excepted. For example, an accident on the way to church)

5. I will be reliable and dependable on my assigned job. Prov. 18:9, further, when I sign up, I will be there to work. Prov. 12:17. Remember, in this church we make 6 month commitments. In 6 months, you can be released unless you decide to "re-enlist".

6. This next point follows #5. I agree to tell my supervisor if I am being used too much, not wait until "burn out" occurs and then quit in anger. Matt. 18:15.

7. I will complete all training even if I have heard it before. Prov. 13:16, 15:5, 15:32, 19:20.

8. I agree to temporarily serve as an exhorter or usher or any other job at any time I am needed during a service.

9. I agree to tithe of my finances and of my time to God. To take time to diligently pray for my family my Church, my Country, my secular job, and all mankind. Heb. 7:1-10 Mal. 3:8-11. Under the New Covenant we can tithe more than 10%. People who aspire to the Helps Ministry must be tithers.

10. I agree to obey the leadership without question during any organized service. The Holy Spirit places leaders in place; I understand that an organized service is an inappropriate place to question authority or anointing. Titus 3:1

11. I agree to take the time to get "prayed up" prior to going on my job so I can be operating supernaturally in the Will of God on my Helps Job. John 14:26

12. As a favor to my Pastor, I agree to accept temporary assignment in another job to fill a need until someone else is found. Three weeks will be the limit of substitutions, not the normal six month commitment.

13. I agree to keep my children under control as an example to other parents, and so mine don't lead others astray. 1 Tim. 3:4

14. To faithfully live and study the Word of God to the best of my ability. To show my self approved and so I can be an example of prosperity and great success. 2:Tim 2:15, Joshua 1:8

I agree to abide by this Code of Conduct as a Helps Worker or staff member of this church.

Signature_____ Date_____

Helps Worker Application _____Church

Last Name_____First_____MI_____

Address_____City_____Zip_____

Day phone_____Cell_____Home_____

1. Are you willing to attend training classes ? _____
2. Are you willing to commit to the ministry for 3 mos_____ 6 mos_____ 1 year_____
3. Indicate your preference for positions by numbering them in the order of preference.

_____Exhorter	_____Youth	_____Lead Home Bible Study
_____Intercessor	_____Singles	_____Weekly Bulletin
_____Usher	_____Young Married	_____Flowers/Altar Guild
_____Nursery	_____Children	_____Senior Citizens
_____Greeter Host/Hostess	_____Bookstore	_____Computer/Powerpoint
_____Illustrating/Art	_____A/V, Sound	_____TV, Satellite
_____Accounting	_____Janitorial	_____Yard/Facility Maint
_____Jail/Prison Ministry	_____Home visitation	_____Nursing home visitation
_____Street Ministry	_____Food/Shelter Ministry	_____Office worker, clerical
_____Bus/Transportation	Other_____	

Sunday School choices: Pre-School/Nursery_____ Elementary Grade_____

Junior High_____ High School_____ Adults_____

Music: Instrument_____ Voice_____

Remarks, any skills you have that can contribute to God's Work in the local church ?
_____
_____
_____

You may be asked to fill in at a position you have not chosen, please bear with us. God will eventually promote you to the job you desire.

_____

Signature

CHAPTER 2

Church Government and Discipline

For years, churchgoers have accused their denominations, leadership, and pastors of "laying bondage" on them when local rules and order were enforced. Cults, such as some of the groups we have heard about on the news, do lay bondage on their members even to death in some instances. You may welcome some people into your church who have had such experiences elsewhere; they must be introduced to church discipline with gentleness and compassion.

Churches also employ associate pastors, office staff, and in larger churches maintenance people, TV and audio professionals, and others who are paid employees. These paid staff must not be forgotten when you teach the Helps Ministry. They must know their function in the local body and what constitutes acceptable performance for the specific jobs they hold.

If your church is denominational and has set procedures for staff, those procedures must be incorporated into your Helps Ministry manual. Most organized ecclesiastical governments are not particularly scriptural. Church governments have to follow the laws and customs of the country in which they minister. They may follow Robert's Rules of Order or other rules of keeping order. In 1 Corinthians 14:40, we read that we must have order and operate diligently. Decently in this context does not mean not cussing; it's more like faithful work habits.

In the ancient tradition, no one voted for a pastor or a prophet, etc. Once, they drew lots from a number of qualified people but did not vote. This is not to suggest that all church governments are bad. If your church votes on pastors, deacons, elders, and so on, don't think I'm suggesting your church is not of God. I didn't say that, and I don't believe that. It's just that if you vote, do it under the unction of the Holy Spirit, not as a method for controlling the church.

If you don't agree with the way your church is governed, pray about it, but do not get into rebellion and criticize your leadership or your denomination. If people want a perfect church, they will have to wait for Jesus to come back. Meanwhile, we will attend the imperfect ones that exist today. You might remind them that if they did find the perfect church, they would not be qualified to join.

Throughout history, God's people have been trying to second-guess Him on how to run His church. Now, we are faced with secular governments that dictate conduct so we can retain our "exempt" church status. We have local governments from whom we must get permission to build or modify our church buildings. Regulations are everywhere. God even has it in His Word; "You do this and I'll do this" is repeated for different promises in the Word. So let's quit griping about it and accept those who have authority over us and follow their instructions. Hebrews 13:17 tells us to take orders from our leaders because they are appointed to watch over us and have to give account for their actions.

God blesses us when we do what He wants us to do, and that is obey His Word; Joshua 1:8 clearly instructs us concerning the Word of God and promises good results for those who follow it diligently.

This chapter will discuss some of the forms of church governments in use today and more important, it will outline some of the scriptures that will give you an appreciation of what God's intentions are. This chapter is instructional in nature; others are organizational and can be modified as the local body sees fit to cover a specific job in a church.

We will discuss the subject of church government a bit differently than you might expect. The basic issue is the challenge of how to run a church in the twenty-first century with a guidebook, the last chapter of which was written almost 2,000 years ago!

There are to precepts we must understood before any serious study of church government can begin. First, Christianity is not a democracy; it is a theocratic form of government. God is sovereign, as evidenced countless times in scripture from Genesis to Revelation. He put it together and gave us free will to operate on earth; we are obligated to the greatest extent to do it His way.

Second, all questions about how to run a church are not answered in the Bible. This sounds simple and obvious, but how many times do we get arguments and church splits about the color of carpeting, chairs vs. pews, or new vs. traditional music? We have rules about placement of the pulpit, dress of the clergy (collars or no collars, etc.) Christians get upset at each other thinking that others are less holy because of their positions on one of these topics or another. This is majoring in minors!

Consider Jesus's earthly ministry, the acts and ministries of the apostles, and the replacement of apostles. They operated under the unction of the Holy Spirit and took instruction from ministers senior to themselves. The congregations did not control the ministers, nor did the ministers control the believers. The fivefold ministry we see in Ephesians 4:11 all refer to people holding office, not a gift of the spirit.

1. apostles
2. prophets
3. evangelists
4. pastors
5. teachers

The above are the ordained (usually) ministers in charge of our local churches now. We need to remember that He gave them to us.

In the United States, most of our churches give some sort of voting privileges to the congregation. This is not biblical, but it exists and will probably not change till Jesus comes back. So let's live with it and when we are called upon to vote, do so only after prayer.

The key to understanding church governance is realizing that there are God's ways, which are not subject to discussion, and local customs and processes, which are. Not letting the local stuff get in the way of our relationship with Jesus is what we are about. Less is best when you're making rules especially when the congregation is concerned. Where workers are concerned, rules are necessary for the good order of the church. Church workers work under the authority of the pastor and the boards; they are responsible for the conduct of the workers and therefore need to have good control over what happens in their names.

There are four variations of church government in the United States; some churches have a blend of these.

Episcopal

The word *episcopal* comes from the Greek *episcopos*, bishop or overseer. In this method of governance, the pastor(s) have a bishop or overseer supervising them; the congregation has little or no say in who its pastor is. The Roman Catholic, Orthodox, Church of England (Episcopal), and Lutheran Churches are examples of this form of government.

The local pastor (priest) has less control over the church. It may not be owned locally. Doctrinal issues are decided by the church through the bishop and probably not subject to question or discussion by the priest or pastor. In some situations, a lay board has some input into some facets of the government and choosing a bishop and pastor. In the United States, traditional roles become confused because of our national custom of the democratic process.

Presbyterian

Presbyterian comes from the Greek *presbuteros*, elder, and *presbuteroi*, the plural. In this form of government, the presbyters or the business leaders of the church have the responsibility to run the church and select a pastor. The Presbyterian Church uses this form of government, and others use variations of it. Sometimes, the Congregational and Presbyterian Churches are almost the same.

Congregational

This is probably the most popular form of church government in the United States. It suits our customs and appeals to our sense of democracy. Here, the congregation (the enrolled members), vote on just about anything you can imagine—buying a church, painting it, adding to it, hiring a pastor, and a myriad of lesser issues. As long as someone wants to vote on it, that person can usually bring it up at a church meeting.

We speculate that since many of our ancestors emigrated from countries in which churches or secular authorities controlled them, they wanted to be free from suppression, repression, and domination, so they came here. This need for control over their destinies carried over to religious worship as well.

This form of government is impossible to justify with scripture, but many great Christian denominations practice this to some degree or another, Assemblies of God, Pentecostal Church of God, most Baptists, Congregational, and Southern Baptists among them. Remember that God gave us ministers (Ephesians 4:11); it seems presumptuous to vote on them. Adherents to these denominations have an enormous responsibility to bathe their votes in prayer. History and church splits have shown us that this form of government frequently pleases the local congregations more than it glorifies God.

Independent

In this form of church governance, pastors can be in control of entire churches and do not answer to boards unless they choose to do so. Elders, deacons, associates, etc. serve at the pastors' pleasure. Examples of this type of government are Moses, who chose his own judges (without a vote) and Old and New Testament prophets, who chose their successors or otherwise operated independently of any authority except God's; none consulted a deacon board or asked the congregation for a vote.

Look into Jesus's ministry; He chose all the disciples, He called the shots, and no one questioned His authority. We see numerous times in scripture where there was disagreement with the edict or teaching of a prophet, but the prophet still stayed a prophet and could not get voted out!

Today, many independent churches are finding that they can trust their pastors and have this form of government. This form is not popular with traditionalists because most mega-ministries and televangelists are organized this way. This form lends itself to abuse by the pastor, so many independent pastors voluntarily answer to lay boards.

There are pastors who, because of custom, familiarity, or no other choice, go along with one of the first three. There is nothing wrong with this. As long as Jesus gets the glory and the true gospel is taught, any form works. Also, many pastors are not taught any sense of business in seminary or Bible school; as such, they are totally unequipped to run the necessary secular business of the church and depend on lay boards for assistance. While this works and exists and probably will not change anytime soon, we must still look to the Bible for God's method of operating a church: "Let all things be done decently and in order" (1 Corinthians 14:40). We make rules and SOPs (standard operating procedures) so things run decently and in an orderly fashion. This includes not just the gifts of the Spirit but also the sound system, the cleanup outside, the ushers, Sunday school, etc.

So let's know and appreciate the forms of government but not get hung up on whether our church is "doing it right." If God gets the glory and the gospel of Jesus is taught, if people get saved and discipled, you are doing it right no matter what form of government you serve under. Let's look to the Bible for some examples we can copy for organizing our churches.

Genesis 1

God created everything in a specific order; what was first had to be first, then the next, etc. He built on the former until He had reformed the earth for Adam. As we organize our local bodies, let's start with the simple and move to the complex. Keep it simple, make it fun and interesting—that's a good motto when we are organizing people.

Genesis 2:20

Adam was charged with naming the beasts so they could be recognized and identified by the population to come. When you put people in charge of tasks, let them "name" the duties; avoid micromanaging. God gave us all brains, so let your trusted workers use theirs. If it is not done exactly how you would have done it, that's okay; *you* didn't have to do it.

Genesis 41:46–47

Joseph carefully organized food storage and prohibited use of it until he said so. When famine came, he had enough for everyone. Very probably, some thought he was being mean or arbitrary, but he was in charge, and history shows us it worked. When allocating church resources, pastors have the last word because they are answerable to God. Advice and counsel of boards or elders is essential, but pastors have to make the decisions biblically. Again, if your constitution says otherwise, don't be condemned—just do your job prayerfully.

Exodus 17:8–16

Aaron and Hur held up Moses's hands during the battle with the Amalekites. When the battles rage, you must hold up your pastors, support their ministries, and defend them from attack.

Exodus 18

Moses was advised to appoint judges to assist him in ruling and to organize in tens, fifties, hundreds, and thousands. Pastors who try to do it all themselves will simply burn out. They are being arrogant if they think they are the only people capable of handling all the tasks necessary to run a modern church. They should learn to delegate.

In 1 Thessalonians 5:12, we are instructed to choose from good people we know, those we can trust, and then delegate, delegate, delegate.

1 Kings 19:16–21

Elisha joined Elijah as his heir apparent to minister to Elijah's needs. Here is our example of finding suitable pastoral candidates and teaching them how to be pastors. We can call them associates, assistants, interns, etc., but we need to always be raising up new leadership.

Ephesians 4

God gave us our preachers as gifts as listed on the second page of this chapter. These people are informally called the fivefold ministry gifts. Their purpose is to edify the saints so the work of the ministry—getting people reconciled with God—can take place. The congregation does the soul winning; the fivefold ministers prepare them to be witnesses and teach them the Word.

Hebrews 13:17

This passage admonishes us to follow the lead of those appointed over us. So no matter what form of government you may serve under, remember that your leadership is there for your benefit and must give account for you. Support them.

1 Thessalonians 5:12

This passage urges us to esteem our leaders highly in love. *Urge* in Greek is more forceful than we may imagine, but it is still from an equal to an equal. It doesn't mean our leaders are better than us, just that they are instructed to lead and we are instructed to follow. Order must be maintained.

1 Peter 5:1–3

The apostle Peter exhorted our pastors and spiritual leaders in this passage to minister to the people in their ministries or congregations as examples of how they are to act. We are leaders training the next generations of leaders. They will learn either good or bad methods depending on how well pastors have fulfilled their biblical charge to be effective and faithful leaders and teachers of the next generation.

It's interesting and informative to look at Jesus's ministry organization: He had a senior staff—Peter, James, and John; He had leadership (the twelve including the senior staff); He had a cadre of officers (the seventy He trained and sent out); He later recharged them (Luke 10:20). He set the example of using multiplication to spread the Word farther. The apostles got the message and went out and made many ministers, then those went out, and it still happens today. Doesn't that bring us back to 1 Corinthians 5:18, in which we learn the term *ministry of reconciliation* by which people are saved?

Concern yourselves with what God puts your hand to in His church. The actual form of government, who is in charge locally, is subordinate to the job you have of getting people in right relationships with the Savior. The church needs to stop majoring in the minors and get on with God's work.

In any well-governed group—whether a church or secular business or government—there is always a chain of command. Someone is ultimately responsible for everything done in the organization. He or she takes credit for the good and is responsible for the bad. In churches, it is the pastor or perhaps the elected board if it is in authority over the pastor.

Serious note to pastors and members: whatever form of operation you have, it is imperative that you have a process of control and discipline. Remember that discipline in a church can be applied only to members who by their signing their memberships agree to abide by the rules and traditions as a condition of membership. Guests or people who attend have made no such promise and cannot be held to membership standards.

Pastors should exhibit strong leadership and stand behind the decisions of their appointed leaders or risk losing those leaders. Many times, leaders who are appointed will have to make uncomfortable choices or decisions that everyone will not agree with. Inevitably, someone will gripe about the difference in opinion to the pastor or church board. (See the discussion on Matthew 18:15 below.)

Leaders who perceive that their decisions can be overruled by the pastor when someone complains will rightly perceive that the pastor does not trust them. Time and again, I have witnessed pastors who in great compassion have overruled a ministry leader to placate a loyal worker. The result was always a loss of respect for the ministry leader by the worker, and ultimately, the leader either quit or ceased to be effective.

Pastors lose if they overrule their leadership because then they have to handle the job they had delegated to someone else. Controlling pastors who fail to delegate authority along with responsibility rarely grow their churches. God will not bring in new members if the pastor refuses to appoint people to assist in filling the many needs of those in their charge.

Pastors cannot do it all and control everything unless their churches are very small. In these cases, pastors do not delegate authority or responsibility. I believe God trusts such pastors with only a small number of members the pastor can control individually. If a pastor recruits and trains leaders but doesn't back them up, that does those leaders a disservice and is a waste of time and resources.

This long-winded "chain of command" discussion is a vitally important subject that needs to be discussed openly and understood by all parties. It is essential that the pastor, the church board, appointed leaders, workers, and the general membership of the church understand the importance that church organization has for the health of the body. This same message has to be conveyed to the congregation in general so they will know the proper biblical process for dealing with differences of opinion.

When there are disagreements, the biblical process is clear: they must discuss their differences of opinion with the person they disagree with first. Jesus made this clear.

> Moreover if your brother sins against you, go and tell him his fault between you and him alone. If he hears you, you have gained your brother. But if he will not hear, take with you one or two more, that "'by the mouth of two or three witnesses every word may be established." And if he refuses to hear them, tell it to the church. But if he refuses even to hear the church, let him be to you like a heathen and a tax collector. (Matthew 18:15–17)

If a member contacts the pastor before discussing it one on one with the leader of the ministry he or she disagrees with, that person is out of biblical order and in sin. End of discussion.

For the purposes of the Helps Ministry and the application of Matthew 18:15, the first person disgruntled ministry members should contact is the leader of the ministry if the leader refuses to listen. Take a witness; go to that leader with another ministry member who agrees with you. If the leader still refuses to make a change, go to the person in the church who is that leader's immediate supervisor, which could be the pastor. In any event, follow the chain of command. An organizational chart posted in the foyer will facilitate this. Everyone must be aware of who reports to whom.

One important note: please check your Bible. If the Bible backs your position, you should share the passage or passages that back your position with your leadership. If the leadership decides to directly violate the Bible, you should leave; if the church is deliberately violating the Bible, you do not need to be there. If the Bible backs the leadership's decision or is silent on the matter, drop the issue and keep praising God in that church.

If the supervisor of that ministry leader agrees with the leader, the discussion ends. If you belong in that ministry, you can make peace with your leader and continue to serve or leave that ministry if the disagreement is serious. Loyal members support their leadership even when they disagree with a decision.

If you are a member of the church and a decision, sermon, or policy is not to your liking, you are obliged to keep quiet; you are not to gossip or bring up the issue with other members of the church. Church members have the same obligation to Matthew 18:15. You go to the person one on one, then with a witness, and then to the church, in this case, a member of the church board. Going to the church does not mean airing your grievance with anyone who will listen.

As long as leaders are operating in a biblical and godly manner, their decisions and modes of operation stand. If workers in a ministry disagree with the operation of the ministry, they must submit as the Bible instructs or leave that ministry. Further, they must remain silent about the situation out of respect for the pastor, who is ultimately responsible for that leader's actions.

Strong pastors will admonish anyone who contacts them before following Matthew 18:15 to go back and do what the Bible says to do first before bringing the matter to the attention of the leader's supervisor. If the pastor is that leader's supervisor, they can then handle the situation only after the complaining party follows Matthew 18:15.

In Ministry of Helps training, the chain of command has to be taught and agreed to by all members. It is very stressful for the pastor to be involved in every dispute in all the ministries of the church. The pastor may have to remove some people from the Ministry of Helps if they persist in coming to the pastor with every perceived problem.

The concept of chain of command is very valuable to pastors in that it solidifies leadership under their pastoral umbrellas. Pastors who respect their leaders' decisions will have leaders who will make the decisions necessary to operate the church decently and in order as required by the Bible. The benefit will be that the pastors will be relieved of all the nit-picking decisions necessary to have a smooth-running church

Will leaders make mistakes? Of course; they're human. But pastors must back up their decisions. God forgives our every sin. In turn, pastors can forgive the occasional lapses of judgment or mistakes of their appointed leadership. One of the prices of delegation is that pastors may have to take the heat for missteps while giving the credit to their ministry leaders when the job is done right.

CHAPTER 3

Training Programs

Each local church should have ongoing training programs for providing members with guidance in every area of ministry. They should be provided with ongoing, up-to-date instruction in their specialties if not locally, then perhaps at regional conferences where they can be made aware of new or improved ways of doing their jobs.

Thorough study and planning should precede any local training. Lesson plans, study materials, overheads, etc. should all be prepared in advance. The pastor and whoever is in charge of training should all be on the same page and in agreement with all that is taught. Instructors should stay with the lesson plans, and the attendees must be sure they learned the material and can competently perform whatever tasks or functions are the topic of the training.

The church world has often put great emphasis on the spiritual classes (Sunday school, ministry schools, etc.) and ignored training on audiovisual, janitorial, office procedures, money counting, and a myriad of other tasks that are mundane but essential to a smooth-running church.

In Matthew 25:21, Jesus complimented someone for being faithful in a little job because that person could be considered for a bigger role. In Luke 16:10, Jesus emphasized that if people handled less-important jobs well, they could be eligible for more responsibility and promotion. That is how we must work in the local church. Test people with less-glamorous jobs to see if they handle them diligently. If so, move them on to more and more responsibility. If they sluff off the less-important jobs, they should not be entrusted with higher offices.

Jesus had a lot to say about being faithful in the small things. Compared with salvation, clean restrooms are a small thing, but to visitors and potential church members, they can be a deal breaker. If you aren't faithful in the small things, how can anyone trust you with the spiritual health of their family?

New people should be supervised closely and trained thoroughly so they can feel confident in their jobs and you can feel confident in their ability to do those jobs. A part of training is publishing job descriptions for each church ministry position. This manual can be your starting point; you can modify it as necessary.

Jesus is our example; He trained the disciples before He sent them out. As we read in the Word, He spent most of His ministry teaching others. We must be no less diligent in training our helpers in the local church.

Whatever method of training you choose, remember 2 Timothy 2:15—we rightly divide the Word of truth.

Training Programs General Information

1. All members should have been through the Ministry of Helps Training Program so they are familiar with salvation, healing, baptism in the Holy Spirit, and the doctrine and government of your church.

2. All workers should receive basic intercessor training so the pastor is sure each of them is competent and comfortable in

    - witnessing and praying someone through to salvation
    - laying on of hands and confidently praying with someone for healing by the stripes of Jesus.
    - witnessing and praying someone through to the baptism in the Holy Spirit
    - being able to cast out spirits from those being oppressed by them

3. They should systematically study the Word of God formally at a Bible college, an online school, or by regular attendance at Bible study group or adult Sunday school in the local church.

4. They should receive specific technical training. In this instance, this will renew their minds with necessary information to effectively do God's work (see Romans 12:2). This data may be worldly, but it will be used to promote God's Word in the local church and community.

5. They should attend teaching credential classes to learn the techniques for preparing lesson plans and organizing them for better understanding by the students.

6. Those aspiring to become teacher should take public-speaking classes. This will teach techniques of delivery, demeanor, and ways of preparing talks so they are easily understood.

7. They should take trade or technical classes for audiovisual/computer techs as necessary. Sometimes, vendors will offer this training free if you use their services for your technical repair and purchases.

8. They should take specific ministry training by local leaders. Having a head of a ministry teach the members is a good idea. It is a great forum for the new folks to ask questions of the leadership. This is not possible with on-the-job training particularly if the job is in the sanctuary on Sunday and the training would disrupt the service.

9. Records should be kept on them so new leaders will know who has been through the program and who has not. Also, hold refresher classes to so members have a chance to give feedback to each other and to the leaders.

An example of the training form is on the next page.

Training Record Form

Name _____

Address _____

Phone _____ Cell _____

E-Mail _____

Date completed Basic Exhorter/Intercessor or Helps class _____

Specific Training in _____ ministry

Educational background
HS grad _____ College _____ years
Major _____ Degree(s) _____ Graduated _____

Other formal Helps training:
Date/Type/Title/School/ Instructor

Application in file? Code of conduct signed?

CHAPTER 4

Intercessory Prayer/Prayer Chain

This short chapter is devoted to the intercessory prayer ministry. This is a ministry that can be the ideal place for those who have little time to devote to the church. Most of their duties will be handled during church services or at home, so there will be no major time commitment for the ministry.

This is an ideal place for people with unsaved members who don't support their church activities. Joining the intercessors gives them a chance to participate in the work of the church without additional resistance from unsaved family members.

Intercessors act as links in the prayer chain ready at a moment's notice to pray for a need in the church. They intercede for the needs of the church by diligent prayer during the week when time permits. In some cases, these folks engage in fervent prayer; read Romans 8:26. These groanings are frequently observed in Pentecostal and Charismatic churches during prayer time when someone appears in agony and pray in intelligible words such as groans or heaves of emotion. This is one of the four kinds of tongues mentioned in the New Testament.

Intercessors' Suggested Procedures

1. Arrive at the service twenty minutes early and save your seat with a coat or a Bible

2. Go to the front of the church and intercede in prayer in the Spirit at the altar. Do not be distracted by musicians and singers getting ready; they will pray with you shortly.

3. Just before the start of the service, lay (join) hands on the pastor and the musicians and uplift them and the service to come. Pray in another room if the sanctuary is used for Sunday school.

4. When numbers of intercessors are sufficient to staff a three-person prayer group, a rotating number of intercessors should pray in the church office or other room during each service. In good weather, you can walk around the church building and intercede.

5. Perform during the week as the prayer chain.

6. Have a notification method whereby the person needing prayer can call the first person in the chain and start the process of notifying everyone else so all can pray in one accord.

7. Make a rule that if the first person does not answer, you call an alternate who will keep the chain unbroken. Rotate the first person on the list and publish his or her name and number in the church bulletin.

8. Dress modestly just as you would for church. No short skirts when up at the altar.

9. Commit yourself to reading the Word daily. Start with one verse and work up from there. Nobody is counting as you and the Lord communicate.

10. Things to pray for.

   - for God to bless your church and all Christians
   - to bind religious and other foul spirits from hindering the service
   - to cast out any other evil spirits from the church
   - for unity in the body of Christ

11. Intercessors are the first group of people to be called to visit people in the hospital or shut-ins. Pastors (especially in large churches) cannot possibly visit every ill or injured church member; the intercessors can and should fill that role.

12. All members should have been through the Ministry of Helps Training Program they are familiar with salvation, healing, baptism in the Holy Spirit, and the doctrine and government of your church.

CHAPTER 5

Ministry of Exhorters (Mistakenly Called Counselors)

In this chapter, exhorters are those who speak with folks who have been ministered to by the speaker or pastor and the speaker or pastor desires that the person be instructed further in the receiving of whatever was ministered to them.

Traditionally, the churches have incorrectly labeled these people as "counselors." This is a legally defined category of licensed professionals in the various states who by education and training have the right to call themselves counselors and have been specifically licensed to counsel others in a specialty. In the church, we refrain from using the term *counselor* to not confuse people or cause anyone to believe we have qualifications we do not.

The Bible is clear: the word *exhorting* is used fourteen to sixteen times in the Old and New King James Versions. The word *counselor* in John refers to the Holy Spirit. In the Revised Standard Version, the word *counselor* appears in John 14:26. In other versions, it reads "comforter." Again, even in that translation the word refers to the Holy Spirit. So let us use the name the Bible does to name those who tell people the gospel they exhort. Hallelujah! Isn't it better to use the God-ordained name for something instead of the world's name?

The Holy Spirit is our counselor, and we Christians exhort the saints under the unction of the Holy Spirit. Unless we are properly licensed, we cannot perform counseling. California's state government and many other governments require specific licensing for drug, alcohol, and family counseling and the like. If you are presented with that sort of problem, refer them to the pastor, who will direct them to the proper place to get professional help.

The word *exhort* appears in 2 Timothy 4:2 and in Titus 1:9, 2:6, 2:9, Hebrews 13:13, and 1 Peter 5:13. This is sufficient evidence that we should be using Bible terminology for witnessing to people about spiritual rather than secular matters. In some jurisdictions, it may even be a violation of law to call yourself a counselor when you aren't licensed by the civil authorities to call yourself one.

This chapter is not is a way of using scripture to get people through psychological or other family situations. Training of that nature is beyond the scope of this manual and is reserved for the professional institutions and seminaries who prepare people to assist in those situations. Volunteer workers in churches do not need this training to be effective exhorters in the biblical context.

What we are charged to do as trained exhorters is to bring scriptures to bear on everyday problems and challenges facing our members and to those to whom we witness. For the power and authority to do this effectively, we use the gift or gifts we have received and outlined in Romans 12:4–8, commonly called the motivational or personality gifts.

Here, we see the exhorter in a biblical context, a Christian operating in obedience to the Word of God. We have these gifts in operation in this chapter and in our churches. Here the example is how we conduct ourselves in church.

We are to exhort the brethren to read the Bible, to live holy lives to the best of their ability, and to attend church. As mentioned again in Hebrews 10:25, we want to get the brother or sister on the right track to living the overcoming life in Jesus Christ.

Remember, anyone can quote scripture. We should seek God's direction through the leading of the Holy Spirit and be prayed up so we can love the person with the Word of God. Faith comes by hearing and clearly understanding the Word of God (Romans 10:17).

People needing the Lord in their lives are sometimes very vulnerable and can be hurt. It is essential that pastors be sure of the qualifications of appointed exhorters before they are allowed to work under the auspices of the local church.

Remember that the Holy Spirit teaches us what we need to know and brings it to our remembrance at just the right time to do what He wants us to do (see John 14:26). Clearly, the only way the Holy Spirit can bring anything to your remembrance is if you have first learned it! We need to study the Word of God to be approved for our jobs in the church

Exhorters' Training and Reports

1. The head of the exhortation ministry should maintain a schedule of who is assigned to work at each service and rotate the members. Male and female exhorters must be in attendance for all organized services of the church; elders can fulfill this role until sufficient people are trained and in place.

2. Dress code usual for the church setting; no shorts, sandals, or wild T-shirts. This is the house of the Lord, and exhorters are to be of clean of body and breath.

3. The head usher should reserve aisle seats for the exhorters on duty so they can quickly get out and up front without disrupting the congregation.

4. During altar calls, exhorters must pay attention to the ushers or head exhorter so they can quickly respond if called up front.

5. The exhorters should take those they are exhorting somewhere quiet so they can engage in conversation, answer questions, and pray with them without disrupting the service or altar call.

6. The exhorters should know what the person just got prayed for at the altar so they can reinforce it privately. Give them a tract or pamphlet about what just took place for them in the service—salvation, healing, etc.

7. Get contact information if they are visitors. Give it to church staff so follow-up can occur to reinforce their good experience with the Lord. Whoever does the follow-up will need this information to make the call and keep in contact with the individual.

8. Before you bring people back into the church if the praying happened at an altar call, be sure to advise them of the follow-up so they can advise you when and how to contact them. Be sensitive. Sometimes, a family member might be hostile to the Lord and follow-up must be done in a way dictated by the individual, not the church.

9. If you are comfortable doing so, give them your information so they can contact you.

10. Suggest they reread the tract and contact you or the pastor if they have any questions.

11. If they are newly saved, suggest that hanging around with Christians will make it easier for them to become involved with the Lord. Unsaved friends, bars, or other unsavory company can cause them to backslide.

12. If they received the baptism in the Holy Spirit, recommend they pray in tongues a few minutes each day. Do it in faith to build them up in the Spirit.

13. If they received healing, explain the difference in healing and an instant miracle. Have them pray thanks to God for their healing and continue to thank God until healing manifests itself bodily.

14. It is availability, not technical qualifications, we are looking for in exhorters, people who will wait on the Lord and study His Word. The Holy Spirit will bring you what you need just when you need it!

15. Listen first. What do these people think about what just happened? What do they want to know? Let them tell you where to go next before you start offering suggestions. They may not have told the person at the altar about everything for which they needed prayer. You must use judgment; it might be prudent to bring them back or just pray for them yourself.

16. Occasionally, a serious problem will come up—child abuse, rape, confession of a crime, etc. These are not problems exhorters should get involved with. They should immediately contact the leader of the exhortation ministry, head usher, or the pastor if the service is over.

    They should not become involved as a confessor or confidant in these situations. Trained, qualified people are the only ones legally and practically qualified to deal with these situations. Many involve serious violations of law, and the authorities must become involved. Satan does enough harm without your becoming involved in some misguided attempt to set things right. Be wise, obey your leaders, and follow these guidelines.

17. The world says, "Have brain engaged before operating mouth." The church says, "Have spirit engaged and controlling brain before operating mouth"; read James 3:8–12.

18. Previously, we suggested highlighting your Bible. Here are some Scripture suggestions. You may have favorites you would prefer to use.

- Salvation: Romans 10:9–10; 2 Corinthians 5:17; Romans 3:23–28, 8:1; Ephesians 2:8–9
- Holy Spirit baptism: Luke 11:13; John 14:16, 17, 26, 16:7; Acts 1:4, 5, 8, 2:38.
- Healing: Isaiah 53:5; Psalm 103:3; 1 Peter 2:24
- Forgiveness: 1 John 1:9; Psalm 51 (scores of these!)
- Casting out demons: Mark 16:17; Luke 9:1, 10:17; John 14:12

19. Make a list of your own a part of your personality. Let God's Word become a part of you. Then the Holy Spirit can bring it to remembrance at just the right moment to help change someone's life!

An exhorter's report/follow-up form, job description for head exhorter, and a sample pastoral letter to be sent to visitors who have received salvation, healing, etc. are on the following pages.

Position Title: Head Exhorter

Accountable to the associate pastor for home groups and follow-up or other leader as locally appointed

Functions

1. During church services and altar calls, this person will be guided by and follow the direction of the head usher and persons ministering at the altar. Their selection, training, and scheduling will be handled by the associate pastor for home groups and follow-up or other leaders as locally appointed.

2. This individual must be a mature Christian as defined in 1 Timothy 3.

3. Head exhorters will supervise the other exhorters and those who follow up after someone has been prayed for at the altar.

4. They will have specific people assigned to every service so there are male and female exhorters at all services.

5. Their duties and responsibilities are assigned pursuant to chapter 5 of the Ministry of Helps manual (attached as appendix I to this manual).

6. They should be members of the teaching team for the Ministry of Helps.

Sample Pastoral Letter (on church letterhead)

Dear _____ (date) _____

We were blessed to have you worship with us on _____. We trust God has blessed you in the days since then. We have regular services on (insert dates and times). You are cordially invited to join us again as we praise God for all His blessings.

We have Sunday school classes available for children and adults and a number of other groups and activities you can take advantage of. They are listed on the enclosed church brochure (if you have one)

If you are interested in joining our church, we have a new covenant believers' class starting soon that will acquaint you with the beliefs we hold and our denominational format and requirements for becoming a member.

We believe we are to love people just the way they are now. God accepts people as soon as they ask Him to do so. We feel the same way. Welcome.

Should you need to speak with me or one of the other pastors (if you have others), please call the church at (phone number) and arrange a conference.

In His love,

(pastor's signature)

Sample Exhorter's Report Form

Form should be Bible sized so some can be carried in the exhorter's Bible at all times. This form should be duplicated and a copy sent to the office and another to the exhorter or follow-up person. Records must be kept of calls and invitations so no one falls through the cracks.

Exhorter's Report

Date_____

Name

Address _____

City _____

Phone _____ E-mail _____

Cell _____

Reason for contact: salvation ___ healing ___ Holy Spirit baptism ___ other _____

Follow-Up Record

_____ assigned to contact during week.

Result _____

Home fellowship leader advised (name) _____

Pastor's welcome letter? (date) _____

Exhorter follow-up call made by (name) _____

Remarks:

CHAPTER 6

Ushers and Altar Calls

Ushers are the most visible of workers during a service. They may take the offering, seat people, serve communion, and be generally more visible to the congregation. Thus, they must represent God, the pastor, and the leadership of the church honorably.

The best ushers are like waiters at a fancy restaurant. They seem to get everything done almost before you ask for it, and they do it in a way that you don't notice how hard they are working. In the church, Jesus gets the glory and the pastor or others ministering from the pulpit get the attention, not the ushers.

The guidelines in this job description will assist you in performing outstanding service to God and the local body. They are not laws to be obeyed; they are a structure we use to ensure everyone is of one accord (Acts 2:1). If we are to expect baptisms in the Holy Spirit and other manifestations of the Spirit in our church, we must be of one accord. Also, instructions reduce the need for decision making, and things run smoother.

1. As with other Ministry of Helps workers, ushers should have been through the Ministry of Helps Training Program so they are familiar with salvation, healing, baptism in the Holy Spirit, and the doctrine and government of your church.

2. Many duties are required: turning on lights, adjusting heat, inspecting bathrooms, etc. Others require the leading of the Holy Spirit and presume the usher is operating supernaturally on the job. An example would be someone throwing a noisy fit during the sermon; when do you remove them? What do you say to them? Where do you take them? You won't find the answers written here. The Holy Spirit must take charge then. Pastors or others in the pulpit may have the unction of the Holy Spirit and give direction, but ushers will do the work and will say the words.

3. Be prayed up, operate in love, and maintain an attitude of a servant, not an enforcer of the rules.

   Fulfill my joy by being like-minded, having the same love, being of one accord, of one mind. Let nothing be done through selfish ambition or conceit, but in lowliness of mind let each esteem others better than himself. Let each of you look out not only for his own interests, but also for the interests of others. (Philippians 2:2–4)

Normal Ushering Duties and Responsibilities

4. Ushers should arrive twenty minutes early; head usher ten minutes before that.

5. They should make sure

    • church is clean and tidy, including bathrooms
    • parking lot, entry, and sidewalks policed
    • A/C or heat properly adjusted
    • proper doors unlocked (or locked)
    • overhead projector readied unless you have an audiovisual ministry
    • offering containers, envelopes, and visitor information cards close at hand
    • water and cups placed for pulpit and musicians
    • tissues and anointing oil at or near the altar area
    • covers or drop cloths available for female altar attendants/ushers

6. They should dress and be groomed to the church's standards.

7. Some may have badges or special coats for ushers so they can be identified.

8. Clean shaven or neat beards. (They should take a vacation from duties while they cultivate beards.)

9. Clean of body and breath. They should use breath mints and deodorant as necessary.

10. They should not come with colds or other attacks of the enemy that might offend or be contagious— especially important when working with children.

11. Ushers should know where all facilities are located. Little facility maps can be duplicated so each usher has one. When someone asks directions of an usher, it is not a good thing to reply, "I don't know."

12. Following the above, a list of all church leaders, the council, and leadership should be made up and given to all ushers so they can point out the correct person when asked and can advise the correct person when a ministry opportunity turns up.

13. They should seat folks in the front seats first so the latecomers do not disrupt the service. Some churches block off the last two rows until the song service is half over.

14. Opening prayer. Sometime after number 1 and prior to the start of the ushers' duties, the head usher should join with the intercessors and perhaps the music people and pray

for the pastor and for needs to be met during the service. The head usher can intercede in the Spirit when not otherwise engaged.

15. They should maintain decency and order in love. During the gifts of the spirit, they should prohibit entry and movement in the service as best they can without being too obvious. They should keep doors closed and have an outside usher keeping people quiet in the foyer.

16. The should pray for crying children, inattentive teens, and full bladders so distractions due to noise and movement are minimized.

17. They should be ready at all times to cast out demons, lay hands on the sick so they may be healed, and for salvation and baptism in the Holy Spirit.

18. They should work inconspicuously; the congregants are supposed to have their attention on the giving of the Word, not the workers.

19. The head usher is usually in charge of the sanctuary when the pastor is in the pulpit. Emergency messages, needs, or gifts of the Holy Spirit for the edification of the church should be presented to the head usher; the head usher should not just let people up to the platform.

20. The pastor and head usher should have prearranged nonverbal signals for use during the service.

21. During services, head ushers lead all ministries. They can direct the activities of any worker. Before and after service, the normal organizational table applies. Head ushers must be sensitive to the other leaders and let them lead their people whenever possible.

22. Sometimes, ushers will be separated from their families during service. Rotate them so it happens as little as possible. When they are with their families, they should not hold babies; they may have to act immediately.

23. The should keep their eyes open even when the pastor says, "All eyes closed." They must be able to spot people fidgeting or raising their hands slightly and point them out to the exhorters or a pastor later. They must guard the assembly from someone who would disrupt during an altar call. They can "get into the Spirit" when they are not needed on the job; that's what rotation is all about.

24. As far as offerings are concerned, they should take a cue from the person in the pulpit. They may want the ushers to clap and stomp in joy at the mention of an offering, or they may want it more dignified. Some pass the bucket or plate; others bring it up front. This

is local option, but it needs to be clear to ushers and congregation alike. (See detailed procedures attached to this chapter.)

25. They will assist in communion. A set procedure must be developed—who comes in early and sets up, who cleans up, and which usher serves the folks on the platform, the audiovisual crew, and the children's church. Lay it out item by item so instructions are clear.. Confusion must not occur during a service.

Altar Calls

26. Altar calls are a specialized part of ushering not done in every church. In major ministries and many prominent evangelists' ministries, we see large altar calls with many ushers acting as directors and "catchers." In the local church, this happens less frequently. However, wise planning suggests that having a written plan in effect and training in operating during an altar call is essential if it is to go smoothly.

27. When you have guest ministers, the head usher should talk with them and get their preferences. If they have none, explain your procedures and get their agreement not to change things in the middle of the service.

28. They should keep lines in order; lines should be only one person deep so catchers can move freely behind them. People waiting should be kept in the aisles and sent to the front as space permits. Once they have been prayed for, they should be guided back to their seats so the altar area will be clear for new folks to come up for ministry.

29. They should let no one touch (lay hands on) the person being prayed for except the minister in charge. The minister will ask for help if needed. They should pray in tongues quietly behind them and watch and listen to the preacher and the person they are behind.

30. Catchers hold at the elbow and small of the back, not the armpits. Armpit catching can ruin your back and your reputation if a male usher's hands slip around the front of a female.

31. A female usher should always be present and instantly place a drop cloth over females preferably on the way down. This takes grace and finesse, but with practice, it can be done easily.

32. The head usher should assign ushers in the rear to control movement and noise.

33. Unless the service has been dismissed from the pulpit, folks should be encouraged to stay in their seats and pray.

Positioning of Ushers

34. Ushers' positions should be numbered, and separate job outlines should be made for each position. Usher 1 is the primary catcher and sits up front; 2 sits on the other side in the front. They are responsible for keeping order on the platform and the primary men catching. Female ushers or other designated females should also be in front for covering duties.

35. Ushers 3 and 4 and higher numbers are situated farther back in the sanctuary.

36. Head ushers will usually stay in the back until the altar call and then move to the front to direct people into the prayer line and supervise the ushers in front. Head ushers will also read signals from the pastor or pulpit minister and advise the prayer team (exhorters) about the needs of the person so after the altar call they can follow up and give encouragement or a tract or a Bible if it is salvation.

37. Outside/parking lot duties are where ushers rotate so they can be with their families during service. Outside ushers have no duties during service, so they are free to get in the Spirit, participate fully in worship, and not be bothered with duties then.

Procedures for Counting the Offerings

38. Always have two or three people count.

39. Rotate the people so the same counters do not always serve together. This prevents ushers from getting too familiar with who is giving and who is not. Also, switching pairs reduces the possibility that the tempter can enter into the process and steal. The head usher should rotate through this detail along with the other ushers and other church leaders.

40. In larger churches, the count should be under the supervision of the church secretary or a board member due to the amounts handled. All people present must sign the Offering Counting Form, a sample of which is attached to this chapter. If a mechanical counting machine is used, an appropriate form should be created locally so at least three witnesses sign for each count.

41. In small groups, only one will collect and a second will stand by and assist in the count.

42. Integrity in handling funds is of paramount importance. The congregation trusts us to collect and safeguard tithes and offerings and use them only for the purposes God intends and that are lawful and proper. Proper audit controls should be in place so there is no appearance of evil or misunderstanding in the use of God's bounty.

43. Make three copies of the Offering Counting Form (at the end of this chapter) and have them available for each offering. One stays in the cash bag, one goes to the pastor, and the third to the church secretary treasurer. The copy given to the secretary treasurer should be filed or scanned and kept on file indefinitely.

Offering Counting Form
(your church name)

Date _____

Event or Service (AM, PM, midweek, etc.) _____

Pennies	_____ @ $0.01	_____
Nickels	_____ @ $0.05	_____
Dimes	_____ @ $0.10	_____
Quarters	_____ @ $0.25	_____
1/2 dollars	_____ @ $0.50	_____
1 dollars	_____ @ $1.00	_____
	Total coins	$ _____

Ones	_____ $1	_____
Twos	_____ $2	_____
Fives	_____ $5	_____
Tens	_____ $10	_____
Twenties	_____ $20	_____
Fifties	_____ $50	_____
Hundreds	_____ $100	_____

Total currency $ _____

Total number of checks _____ Total amount of those checks $ _____

Total Offering $ _____

Counter _____

Counter _____

Counter _____

Three copies: one with deposit, one to pastor, one to church secretary treasurer

CHAPTER 7

Sunday School and Children's Church

We learn why we have children's programs in the church in Proverbs 22:6: "Train up a child in the way he should go, And when he is old he will not depart from it."

All classes, whether for children or other ages, should be conducted with the same careful preparation and honor God in the same way pastors conduct church services. There must be purpose and structure, a beginning, middle, and summation that calls the students to godly action.

Children's church should be a copy of the adult church to train the children about ushers, about order, and being attentive to the speaker. The difference with children is that they may be allowed to ask questions during their service, but they must be instructed that in adult services, questions are not allowed.

Match the duties and responsibilities of the children serving as ushers or altar workers to their ages and levels of maturity; don't expect them to quickly attain adult capability. They are after all kids. We let them "practice" church as children so they know what to expect and how to conduct themselves when they are in adult church.

We learn the importance of Sunday school to renew people's minds in Romans 12:2: "And do not be conformed to this world, but be transformed by the renewing of your mind, that you may prove what is that good and acceptable and perfect will of God."

Organized classes may be the only effective way to make sure that minds are being reached so they can be renewed. Teachers must provide innovative and interesting ways to accomplish this. The world uses junk TV, junk magazines, and all manner of contests, promotions, and advertising to get us to purchase certain products.

Jesus used amazing miracles and lived out a life of love and caring. His messages were short and to the point. Read Matthew 5:30–7:26, the Sermon on the Mount, aloud. Time yourself. Jesus said a lot in a short time. We must strive as teachers to present timely, interesting material that informs and encourages listeners to take action for God and to equip them to tell others about Jesus. We want to equip them to have answers to difficult Bible passages and have biblically sound answers as to why good things happen to bad people and bad things sometimes happen to good folks.

The Devil is competing for the hearts and minds of our children, our members, and for the world at large. We must have alternative information—the truth of the Word of God—to counter his attempts to distract the world and Christians too.

General Requirements for These Ministries

1. All teachers should be vetted by the denomination or the leadership if you are an independent church. There are services that will do background checks utilizing fingerprints to determine if people have records that would preclude them from interacting with children. Some denominations require all teachers to have police background checks before they are allowed to conduct classes. I suggest that *all* workers be screened.

2. All members should have been through the Ministry of Helps Training Program so they have familiarity with salvation, healing, baptism in the Holy Spirit, and the doctrine and government of your church.

Checking Backgrounds

3. This is a real problem; being timid about doing background checks or overly sensitive to people not wanting to provide their birth date, etc., is dangerous.

4. Those who do not want to participate in getting their backgrounds checked must be lovingly and gently informed that they are will not be allowed to participate in ministry under the auspices or the covering of the church. The legal liability ramifications are too serious to make exceptions because someone is sensitive about his or her age or does not want to provide a Social Security number or be fingerprinted. If you relent on this requirement and the person does something bad, the church can be held legally liable for not requiring this person to be vetted when everyone else was checked out.

Personnel Selection

5. It is good practice to have tryouts for teachers. Have potential teachers conduct classes for the pastor and leaders and evaluate their delivery, their use of language, and generally their ability to bring forth the Word. You're not looking for professionals but for those who are willing to put themselves in an uncomfortable situation and still get the message across. Finding good Sunday school teachers is a challenge.

6. Participation in this ministry requires a higher level of commitment than for other Helps workers due to the extra time needed to prepare for classes and the fact that teachers have to show up for every class. Also, most teachers must commit to a longer time, usually a year, so there is continuity in the class.

7. Require formal church membership. Make sure the candidates are committed to your local church, support your vision, and are regular attendees and tithers. As must pastors and other leaders, teachers must set the example of commitment and a Christian lifestyle.

8. All Sunday school teachers should be involved in some sort of continuing Christian education. The can attend a Bible school, take classes online, or participate in a home study group. I was in a church where the pastor held classes for his home study/Sunday school people; that way, he had firsthand knowledge of each of them and was able to influence the teaching provided to his congregation. This activity will bring great blessing into your life.

Structure Ideas for the Classes

9. Children's church should be conducted much the same as regular church services. Classes, however, should be tailored to the ages and attention span of the attendees.

10. Classes for adults and teens who attend the regular service should be just that, a class. Questions should be invited and discussions led by the teacher. Teachers must keep the discussion on topic and not let a single student dominate the conversation.

    *   opening prayer
    *   brief review of the last class if it is a series
    *   presentation of the lesson plan
    *   explanation of what will be presented
    *   presentation of the lesson from a written lesson plan
    *   explanation of what was presented—a brief review
    *   mention of the next week's program and topic
    *   closing prayer and dismissal (always on time)

11. The classes should follow a planned track so the process of going from children's classes to teen classes and then to adult classes will progressively reveal God's Word in a unified way and students aren't confused by conflicting opinions.

Class Materials

12. All material used for any Sunday school class must be carefully reviewed by the Sunday school superintendent and approved by the pastor.

13. If standardized lesson plans are purchased, teachers must present them as they are written. If they create their own, they must be approved.

14. Material must be based on scripture, not opinion (see Galatians 1:8).

General Instructions

15. Emphasize that the Bible is the final authority and the guidebook for their lives.

16. Present Christianity as a way of life, not just religion to be "practiced" on Sunday.

17. In Proverbs 4:20, God made some points we should bring to the attention of students.

    - Listen attentively to and read the Word.
    - Remember the scriptures as they bring life and health to us.
    - Don't talk coarsely or meaninglessly.
    - Don't look at perverse things; keep your eyes on God.
    - Walk in the ways of the Lord. Walk straight and refrain from evil.

18. Let's eliminate denominational prejudice in our children and teach them that all churches that teach Jesus Christ are okay. "But Jesus said, 'Do not forbid him, for no one who works a miracle in My name can soon afterward speak evil of Me. For he who is not against us is on our side" (Mark 9:39–40). When Jesus said that a person who was doing His will in a manner different from what one of the disciples did, that was okay. So if another denomination meets on a different day of the week or uses wine instead of grape juice for communion or sprinkles instead of immerses, cut its members some slack. If they love Jesus and preach Him risen, don't sweat the small stuff. Our job is to reconcile the world to Jesus, not criticize other Christians.

Recommendations Regarding Ministry Members

19. Dress and grooming. Always be clean of body and breath. You are serving in a pastor-like role for the students. Conduct yourself accordingly.

20. Have trained substitutes and rotate them into the schedule so they are comfortable taking over when you go on vacation or are unable to make a class. Make sure all teachers take a break and offer their substitutes a chance to get experience. New teachers are groomed this way; ease them into a place where they are comfortable making a longer-term commitment. This keeps the regular teachers from burnout when they are stuck and there is no backup.

21. Discipline. With God's help, we must overcome the world's perception of harsh, overly legalistic Christians. Jesus's example of love must be ours. We must keep order in all the classes out of respect for the students. Order must be maintained in love but firmly and without favoritism.

22. Teaching methods vary by age group and by the abilities of the teacher. Sunday school leaders must seek God's leading to match proper teachers with appropriate age groups. Some teachers may have a preference, and that must be considered. Your students are not guinea pigs for experimenting with teaching techniques. Stick to approved lesson plans, use teaching aids where needed—movies, skits, and discussions are all options.

Some Ideas for Interesting Children

23. Puppets. Complementing/emphasizing the good guys and chastising the bad guys and then restoring them with godly forgiveness. This can be done in a fun and entertaining way.

24. Songs are a good way to memorize scripture. Sing the scripture, and it is easier for the children to remember words when they sing them.

25. Felt boards, chalkboards, crayons, etc. are not used just for amusement but because children are familiar with them. Put them to use proclaiming God's Word, not just to occupy children's time.

26. Memorizing verses for group recitations should be used so the Word will become imprinted on the thoughts and spirits of the children.

27. Moving in the gifts of the Spirit. This can and should occur in children's ministry. However, teachers should be very vigilant that it is the Spirit of God in operation, not children copying what they have seen others do in church. This is not easy; teachers have to be "prayed up" and sensitive to the Spirit. We must not quench the supernatural operation of the gifts, so we should pray for discernment in this area. Instruction on the gifts and explaining the differences in the gifts of the Spirit is essential. It follows that the teachers must be thoroughly familiar with the gifts and their use. There are four types of tongues revealed to us in the Word of God.

    - First: A way to speak with God, or tongues for personal edification (see 1 Corinthians 14:2, 4, 14; Jude 20).
    - Second: Tongues spoken in church for interpretation, for exhortation, or as a sign for the unbeliever (1 Corinthians 14:22, 26–28).
    - Third: Tongues as a supernatural gift of speaking in a regular language you never learned. This happened at Pentecost when the visitors to Jerusalem heard the newly Spirit-baptized believers speaking in the listeners' native languages (Acts 2:4–6).
    - Fourth: Groanings that cannot be uttered. This is a manner of praying in situations that we are so overcome we cannot think of the appropriate words. The Spirit gives utterance here; we have no control of what comes out of our mouths (Romans 8:26).

28. Teachers should know the difference in the ministerial gifts given to the church in Ephesians 4:11; very few people in a congregation will fall into this group. However, everyone in church will have a gift mentioned in Romans, for these gifts are given to all Christians (Romans 12:2–7). They are commonly called the motivational or foundational gifts. They could also be called personality gifts. The reason is because how we move in the gifts God gives will be how others perceive us and to an extent how we perceive

ourselves. How others move in their gifts will influence how we witness to them or teach them in Sunday school. Remember Romans 12:2: "each according to the measure of faith God apportioned."

29. Printed material is available online and through your denomination or a Bible bookstore. Printing it yourself can work if the teacher has lessons that the leadership has approved. All locally generated programs must be biblically sound and conform to denominational guidelines.

On the following pages are job descriptions for Sunday school superintendent, Sunday school teachers, secretary treasurer of the Sunday school, and a money-counting procedure.

Position Title: Sunday School Superintendent

Reports to _____ (insert the position this individual reports to)

Functions

1. Serves as the executive head of the Sunday school department (see your bylaws and insert the authority in your bylaws for this position)

2. Shall be nominated by the church advisory committee and ratified by a vote of the church membership at the annual business meeting

3. Presides over planning and other meetings for Sunday school

4. Supervises the assistant superintendent, secretary treasurer, teachers, and the children's church conducted during regular services

5. Is responsible to make sure that all Sunday school workers receive copies of the bylaws and written instructions that outline the duties and responsibilities of the departments

6. This person must have proper clearances to work with children—fingerprints and police clearance in the process approved by the denomination or private clearance contractor

7. Must be a regular tithing member of (insert your church name)

8. Must have completed the Ministry of Helps Training Program

Position Title: Secretary Treasurer of the Sunday School
Reports to the Sunday school superintendent

Functions

1. Shall be nominated by the church advisory committee and ratified by a vote of the church membership at the annual business meeting

2. Keeps accurate records of enrollment and attendance

3. Keeps notes and minutes at meetings of the Sunday school department

4. Orders and distributes Sunday school supplies

5. Prepares and submits the annual checkup to the district Sunday school director

6. Is responsible for all Sunday school funds and shall deposit them with the church secretary treasurer, who writes all checks for Sunday school purchases. Proper money counting process will be used (form attached)

7. Keeps an itemized accounting of receipts and disbursements for Sunday school business and files it with the church secretary treasurer

8. Must be a regular tithing member of (insert your church name)

9. Must have completed the Ministry of Helps Training Program

Position Title: Children's Church Director
Reports to the Sunday school superintendent

Functions

1. In charge of the children's church during morning worship

2. Is appointed for the school year starting March 1 by the church advisory board

3. Shall make a plan for how the services will be conducted and have that plan approved by the Sunday school superintendent

4. Must have proper clearances to work with children—fingerprints and police clearance in the process approved by the (insert your church name)

5. Other duties as the Sunday school superintendent may assign

6. Must be a regular tithing member of (insert your church name)

7. Must have completed the Ministry of Helps Training Program

Position Title: Sunday School Teacher

Reports to the Sunday school superintendent

Functions

1. Teaches the class assigned to them—adult, children, youth, etc.

2. Appointed by the executive committee for the school year starting March 1 each year.

3. Curriculum must be approved by the executive committee before materials are purchased, or if written by the teacher, approved by the pastor before it is presented to any class.

4. Pursuant to the bylaws, a teacher may not have more than (to be determined locally) number of unexcused absences in the Sunday school year. (We cannot have classes without a teacher because someone just failed to show up!)

5. Teachers must have proper clearances to work with children—fingerprints and police clearance in the process approved by (insert your church name).

6. Teachers must be a regular tithing member of (insert your church name).

7. Teachers must have completed the Ministry of Helps Training Program.

Offering Counting Form
(your church name)

Date _____

Event or Service (AM, PM, midweek, etc.) _____

Pennies	_____ @ $0.01	_____
Nickels	_____ @ $0.05	_____
Dimes	_____ @ $0.10	_____
Quarters	_____ @ $0.25	_____
1/2 dollars	_____ @ $0.50	_____
1 dollars	_____ @ $1.00	_____
	Total coins	$ _____

Ones	_____ $1	_____
Twos	_____ $2	_____
Fives	_____ $5	_____
Tens	_____ $10	_____
Twenties	_____ $20	_____
Fifties	_____ $50	_____
Hundreds	_____ $100	_____

Total currency $ _____

Total number of checks _____ Total amount of those checks $ _____

Total Offering $ _____

Total Offering $ _____

Counter _____

Counter _____

Counter _____

Three copies: one with deposit, one to pastor, one to church secretary treasurer

CHAPTER 8

Nursery and Preschool

These children have special needs; their attention span is very short. Accordingly, the programs should be short and attractive to young eyes. Popular children's TV programs feature a lot of rhyming and sing-along. This is simply repetition, and children learn to memorize the alphabet and numbers in this manner. We can use this to teach Bible verses and simple Bible stories by rhyme and by singing Bible stories.

Remember that the Word does not return void but does what God intends it to do even in the minds of little children (see Isaiah 55:11).

There is a lot of material online and in Christian bookstores that teaches young listeners Bible stories and verses. If they can sing along with TV commercials and convince their parents to buy some product or another, surely we can offer good Christian content for them to sing along with and talk to their parents about.

Worker Selection

1. All workers in this ministry must have passed police background checks. These are available through major denominations or from private sources at reasonable cost. Churches must protect themselves from criticism that will invariably result after an incident of molestation by a church representative and it is found that no background check was performed. You must have all the members of these ministries checked out to protect the innocent lives entrusted to the local church.

2. All members of this ministry must have undergone Ministry of Helps training so they are familiar with the scriptures for salvation, Holy Spirit baptism, and healing. They must be ready and in season to witness to their charges in language and manner appropriate to their ages.

3. These workers are not just babysitters; they have to be committed Christians able to minister the Word to children and the children's parents as necessary.

Ministry Duties List
(Not all-inclusive; make your own and stick to it)

4. All workers should arrive half an hour early and make sure the facilities are clean.

5. They should dress and groom appropriately for the job; easily cleaned clothes are a good bet as children can be messy.

6. They should be clean of body and breath.

7. Have a sign in/out system so you keep track of which child goes with which parent. Do not release a child *except* to a parent *unless* you have signed parental permission to release the child to another person. Have a form for this purpose and use them.

8. Refuse to receive an obviously sick child. You cannot jeopardize the health of all the other children to take in a sick child. Some immature or misguided parent might try to game the system, you must stand firm, and the pastor must stand ready to back up the decision of the children's ministry worker.

9. Pray over the children and stay calm when they get boisterous. Rebuke spirits of fear quietly and be sure to pray over the room before the day begins. Ask God's blessing on the children and on the workers.

10. Sing Word songs, psalms, or play recordings of children's Christian music

11. Have adequate supplies of diapers (in case a parent forgets) and antibiotic wiping cloths to be used to clean toys and furnishings frequently. Also tissues for wiping runny noses.

Programs

12. First, keep them simple and short—their attention spans are.

13. Content should be fun to get the kids involved. Be visual and repetitive.

14. Have a plan for the day's activities; deciding what to do after you get there is usually the road to failure. Have your supplies ready so the kids don't have to wait and get into mischief while you retrieve a prop or visual aid. You may not always stick to the plan, but having one will give you a guide to keep things on track.

15. Remember that the Word will not come back void. Be diligent, bring content that glorifies God, and stay faithful to the Bible. Yours is a very important job, and it is crucial to the futures of the children in your charge. You never know what the Word of God that you have spoken over them will accomplish in children's lives.

CHAPTER 9

Greeters and Hosts

These two jobs will probably be combined in a small church but will be separate ministries in larger churches. In either case, all members should have been through the Ministry of Helps Training Program so they have familiarity with salvation, healing, baptism in the Holy Spirit, and the doctrine and government of your church.

Members of these ministries will be the "social" people, folks who reach out in friendship as a part of their personalities—outgoing, not shy. Most are attracted to this ministry because there is little time commitment, and when they are "working," it's more like socializing. This is an excellent ministry for those who like to plan parties and fun events.

Greeters function at the church door and greet (and hug if appropriate) people as they enter. They introduce themselves and welcome members and guests. They should make an effort to remember names and greet by name if possible. Greeters should also be working at picnics, potlucks, and any other official church functions to greet all attendees.

Greeters are also responsible to hand out visitor cards and brochures to new people. Some pastors like to do this during the service so they can welcome guests. Just decide on a way of doing it and stick to it.

Greeters may be assigned to follow up on guest registration cards and contact them during the next week and invite them back. The information on the card should go to the church office so a welcome letter can be signed by the pastor. This should be done by the next Tuesday at the latest.

Some churches may have hosts do the follow-up. Just decide who is responsible and the ministry leader should check to make sure all people were contacted. A report should be forwarded to the pastor by the ministry leader containing the names and contact numbers of the people contacted and the results of the conversation.

Copies of the pastor's letter and the contact card should be maintained by the ministry leader and further follow-up initiated in the coming weeks. Records of all contact should be kept for each visitor; no one should fall through the cracks. Many potential church members are lost because they perceived that no one cared about them enough to acknowledge their presence or invite them back.

Normal Greeters' Duties

1. Greeters should arrive half an hour before service to greet other workers and early arrivals. They should intercede in the Spirit as they work. It is best if you have enough greeters to have two or three people at each door so you can have a number of lines going in at all times.

2. A dress code should be established for this ministry. They are out front, so being well dressed and groomed is a necessity. Dress codes are local options, but don't intimidate guests with fancy clothes or jewelry or turn them off with shabby attire.

3. They should be on the lookout for people with needs; some will have them written all over their faces. Greeters should introduce them to an exhorter or usher who can take more time to perhaps help them.

4. They should leave their personal concerns at home and be ready to minister to other people's needs with a loving attitude right at the door.

5. They should know the layout of the church and surrounding area so they can give directions and the names of the people there such as the directors of the nursery or the Sunday school.

6. Greeters should pass out church bulletins to everyone, even the kids. They may mark them up, but some will find their way home and remind the parents about the church and hopefully read the Bible passage contained in that week's bulletin!

7. This ministry may be responsible for duplicating the bulletins, but they should collect and organize all the literature, brochures, etc. that are handed to new guests. This information should include information about the church or denomination, a background and photo of the pastor and family, and a clear statement of faith so the visitors know exactly the core beliefs of the church. This should include scheduled meetings of the church, locations and times of home Bible study groups, youth activities, children's facilities, and other information about the local church and its ministries. This can include other interesting data about the area that you might like to pass out so the guests know you have truly thought about them and are trying to make them feel welcomed and needed.

8. On special days, have flowers to pass out to the women.

9. They should have nametags with their names writ large so everyone can read them easily and call them by name.

Hosts' Duties

1. Hosts are the party planners. They make lists of who is bringing what to potlucks, arrange publicity, make posters, and even write up press releases for the media for big events.

2. Hosts will be in charge of refreshments (if they are provided) for guests at every service. They can solicit donations of snacks from members on a rotation basis or (finances permitting) buy them and be reimbursed by the church.

3. Hosts can be in charge of new converts' "birthday" parties. When people get saved in the church, the hosts should provide them Bibles with their new birthdays commemorated in writing. If the pastor can sign them, that's a bonus, but someone in this ministry should give each a Bible.

4. Hosts can take care of guest ministers and provide for their needs. That can include making hotel reservations as needed and ensuring that the church pays for that as well as meals at restaurants If that was the arrangement.

5. Arrange for meals at the homes of members (and scheduling them so everyone knows who is the host family for that meal) or at restaurants. Some churches provide accounts at local restaurants so the visitors can eat and put it on the church's tab.

6. If funds are available, the host ministry should have flowers delivered to the female minister or the wife of a male speaker at the motel.

7. Hosts should provide guest speakers or ministers a schedule of the times and places of services and any meetings, whom their contacts are, and their cell phone numbers, the pastor's contact numbers, and other relevant information for their visits. (A sample format is at the end of this chapter.)

8. Hosts should arrange transportation (line up cars and drivers and backup cars and drivers) for guests if needed.

9. Hosts should make sure guests know when and where they will receive their honoraria or offerings, though the pastor will usually handle that. This should also be outlined in a letter from the pastor to the guest minister and sent well in advance of their visit. (A sample format is at the end of this chapter.)

10. Hosts will have the guests meet with the pastor and ministry leaders to outline any special needs they may have—music, audiovisual, musical equipment, instruments, etc.

11. They will coordinate with the head usher on how altar calls are to be handled.

12. They will coordinate with the head greeter on help with the guests' book table if that is needed.

13. Hosts will handle any other situations or details specific to that guest minister.

Position Title: Hospitality Leader

Accountable to the pastor or other person in charge of the Helps Ministry

Functions

1. Responsible for four areas of ministry. Must appoint people to do these jobs and make sure they are done. Initially, the leader will be involved in all these ministries; as you grow, there will need to be three assistants assigned to these tasks.

   - Kitchen staff. A leader or husband-and-wife team assisted by a number of selected volunteers. Each must be briefed on the operation of the kitchen equipment and its maintenance. Instruction sheets and checklists must be developed. Cleanup instructions and sign-off sheets for the last user must be used. We do not want anyone becoming sick because of poor hygiene.

   - Food pantry. This leader must head up the donations of food and the distribution of food to needy families.

   - Host ministry, guest speaker accommodations. This is very important. Some visiting speakers require housing, meals, and transportation, and they should be treated as the visiting dignitaries they are. Detailed expense vouchers must be made out for each guest so you can track expenses and know that all monies were handled as godly stewards should do.

   - Greeters' ministry, including after-service receptions. As needed or requested, hospitality leaders will arrange for receptions after the worship services during which the pastor and elders can meet privately with visitors.

Sample Guest Speaker Letter of Understanding

(Sent over the pastor's signature in advance of the guest minister's visit.)

Date
Name
Address
City, State

Dear Rev. _____

We are pleased that you have accepted our invitation to speak at our church on (insert dates and times) we are located at (your address). As we discussed on the phone, I understand you will need following equipment and assistance: (list all agreed-upon needs or equipment or assistance here so there is no question of what they asked for and what you are providing).

Reservations have been made at (give address and phone number of hotel or motel and check in and out times or attach the reservation sheet for their information). We have (or have not as appropriate) prepaid your stay for (the number of) nights. There is a restaurant on premises, and you can charge your meals to your room; we will be paying all your room and meal expenses.

I would like you to join my family for (note meal and date). Other members of the church would like to host your visit and will be contacting you when you arrive. If you wish to take your meals privately to have some quiet time, advise your hosts (names) and they will make sure you are not disturbed. Your privacy will be respected and you are not obligated to accept invitations as a condition of your visit.

A laborer is worthy of his hire. Luke 10:17. A hundred percent of all offerings will be accounted for and paid to you. We enjoy blessing our guest speakers. (Payment terms should be clearly stated in this letter and adhered to by staff.) At the close of the final service, I will give you a check from the church account for all monies collected on your behalf. (If the motel and restaurant bills are to be subtracted from the payment, that should be noted; otherwise, *all* offerings collected for the guest minister must be paid to them.)

Thank you again, and we look forward to your visit and the movement of the Spirit that will occur in the meetings.

(close and pastor's signature)

Sample guest speaker local information form

Name of church
Address, city, state, zip code

Local information for _____ (name of guest speaker) and list of people assigned to assist you during your visit welcome to our city.

Transportation

Primary_____ telephone/cell_____

Backup _____ telephone/cell_____

Hospitality, accommodations, meals

Primary _____ telephone/cell_____

Backup _____ telephone/cell_____

Pastor's name _____ telephone/cell_____

Head usher's name_____ telephone/cell_____

Head exhorter's name_____ telephone, cell_____

Our office is at (address). Your accommodations are at the (name of motel or hotel and its phone number). We are committed to making your visit a blessing to you and our congregation. Please call one of the above listed people should you need anything during your stay. Please make any comments on the reverse side you think of that we can do to improve our service. If you get it to the pastor, we will make any corrections. Thank you for helping us do a better job.

(You may have local input to change or modify this sheet to suit your specific needs.)

CHAPTER 10

New Members' Class

Most denominations and many independent churches have specific formats for admitting new members. This manual presents a suggested methodology and should be modified to reflect denominational or local preferences. The important thing is that the class should be standardized so each class gets the same information and the same rules, customs, and processes and everyone will be on the same page.

This class (or series of classes) is extremely important to the local body because you need to get to know those you are admitting into formal membership and all the benefits (including voting) that membership confers. In all churches, particularly large ones, it will be the only time the pastor or associates interact with the church members on a personal basis.

During these classes, the pastor introduces all the ministries of the church including home groups, other social groups, and children's activities. The pastor can answer questions and perhaps interest the new person in participation in one or another of the opportunities offered in that body.

Typically, churches offer these classes on an as-needed basis, but scheduling meetings and inviting the congregation to bring in new people can help a church grow. A list should be kept in the church office of those indicating a desire to join. The pastor should start a class to accommodate these people so they do not have to wait an extraordinary time to become members.

In 1 Corinthians 1:10, we are admonished to speak in one accord. The class has to be structured to clearly outline the tenets of the faith, denominational rules, and local rules and customs so people feel a part of the body and not wonder what's happening all the time. Being ignorant of local customs and denominational differences can lead to confusion and embarrassment. We cannot control when a guest makes an error, but we can inform our membership so they do not subject themselves to correction.

Texts and Materials Needed

1. Copies of the church constitution and bylaws should be passed out at the first meeting.

2. Copies of the denomination's or local church's statement of faith should also be passed out at the first meeting.

3. A list of all ministries of the local church with the names and contact information for the leader of that ministry should be passed out at the meeting(s) during which the ministries of the local church are spoken about.

4. A copy of the membership roster (so they have the names of all members and can learn who is who) is passed out when they complete the classes and agree to become members. This information is not given out to the public since it has all the members' personal contact information.

5. Class theme: I am a Christian and choose to practice my Christian walk in the (insert your church name). If ever there is a conflict between what I hear at this church and what is written in the Bible, I will choose God and believe in His Bible.

Some of the Things New Members Agree to Do

6. I'll pray for others, including leaders, not criticize them.

7. I'll pray and work to resolve apparent differences in what I have been taught and what this church believes, not criticize and cause strife.

    (Let them know that the pastor or other leader is available to explain things in detail and give the member peace. There are many small differences in denominational practice; these man-made differences usually do not conflict with the Bible and can be resolved without strife.)

8. I believe that my secular life will be blessed by living the best Christian life I can. If I can demonstrate honesty, truthfulness, loyalty, obedience to leaders, and creativity, these traits will be appreciated by employers and others.

9. I will rebuke the Devil when he vainly attempts to put sickness, discouragement, or strife or any negative thing in my life.

Teachings

This is an abbreviated list. You will have to add or delete items to conform to your denominational or local teachings.

10. The Bible is our only sacred book; it is the infallible Word of God. Despite differences in translations and language, the message is the same. Jesus is Lord, and His core teachings do not vary with the translation or the language the Bible is printed in.

11. Other churches or denominations may emphasize or teach different interpretations of the Bible. We must not criticize them or speak ill of them for their differing beliefs.

12. Romans 8:1 teaches us that there is no condemnation to those who believe in the Lord Jesus Christ. It is not our job to condemn them because we think they are "off" in their Christian walk or understanding of the Word.

13. Mark 9:38–41 teaches us that if they are not against us, they must be for us regardless of their differing practices. Let us speak well of all Christians who love Jesus and consider Him Lord. Let's rid the church of religious prejudice; there is enough of that in the world. Others don't need us to be prejudiced too!

14. According to Hebrews 1:1–4, Jesus's sacrifice was sufficient for all.

15. Teach the confession principle of mountains moving by faith in Mark 11:23–24 and Matthew 17:20.

16. Emphasize the law of seed time and harvest as cited in Genesis 1:12, Mark 4:14, and Luke 6:38. When you give, it is a blessing to God and to you.

How We Worship

17. In music—Psalm 33:2–3, Ephesians 5:19

18. By raising hands—1 Timothy 2:8, Psalm 134:2

19. By clapping hands and shouting—Psalm 47:1

20. In dancing—Psalm 149:3

21. By falling in the Spirit—Daniel 10:17, John 18, where the Holy Spirit caused people to fall.

22. By moving in the spiritual gifts—1 Corinthians 12

23. By speaking in one accord—1 Corinthians 1:10

24. By preaching the Word as the apostles did it and no one else—Galatians 1:8

25. By baptism—Matthew 28:19

26. By receiving communion—Matthew 26:26–28, Mark 14:22–24, Luke 22:19, 1 Corinthians 11:23–30

27. By dedicating our children, common among Jews and practiced by Jesus—Matthew 19:13–15

Suggestions for New Believers

28. Make gradual changes in your lifestyles; substitute the things of God for those worldly things that sometimes just waste time.

29. Get up a little earlier each morning and read God's Word before you start your day. Easy to do, and takes only a few minutes of your time. Hopefully, you will get interested in increasing your reading time to a chapter a day.

30. Make notes so you can ask another Christian or leader when you have questions.

31. Join other Christians in Bible study or other spiritual activities. Wean yourself of your unsaved acquaintances who might lead you down the wrong path.

32. Set aside some time to pray. Pray with your spouse. Men should be the spiritual leaders of their family and set the example for the children.

Important Notes

33. New converts to Christianity and people who were hurt in other churches may be spiritually starved. They are vulnerable to false teaching and may not believe everything you say. Stick close to scripture!

34. Clearly explain the concepts and precepts you follow that are nonnegotiable mandates from God and those that are local or denominational rules or customs thus subject to change.

35. Show that your rules and customs are for local order and they are expected to be followed, but at all times they are subordinate to God's Word and never will be in conflict with it.

36. We follow traditions and customs because they seem to have a stabilizing effect on an organization or group of people. They impart a feeling of being part of something special. They also give order. We know what time to show up, how to dress, when to talk, and when to stay silent and listen. Rules and traditions give structure and order to life and make us feel comfortable.

37. In Mark 7:1–23, Jesus gave a long discourse on traditions versus God's teachings. There is a place for both, but Jesus taught that too much emphasis on traditions as the Pharisees practiced is a bad thing.

CHAPTER 11

Music Ministry

This ministry is an important part of any worship service and a blessing to a local church. The members of this ministry not only minister at services and events but also can be ambassadors for Christ to the local community by performing at events and celebrations sponsored by others.

Singers and musicians frequently have performed in the "world" and may have highly developed technical skills sometimes eclipsing their spiritual walks. They have the ability to skillfully arrange, organize a musical group, train musicians, and a myriad of other musical and entertainment skills. Many times, these skills will be more developed than those of the existing staff and leadership.

The music minister must be a strong leader but does not have to be the most skilled musician. Their role is to lead in worship, and the musicians and singers are participants assisting that leader in leading the congregation in an attitude of worship. A sanctuary musician's function is to prepare the congregation for worship, to minister in song, and to be psalmists, not entertainers.

Good music attracts the unsaved and leads the saved into a closer walk with God.

Personnel Selection

1. Select a ministry head with strong leadership abilities, if possible, an associate pastor, so he or she has spiritual authority in the church. It is helpful if the leader has good musical skills too. (See the job description at the end of this chapter.) Think of a symphony conductor who might not be able to play all the instruments but can lead others who can.

2. All members must be regular tithing members of the congregation.

3. All members should have been through the Ministry of Helps Training Program so they have familiarity with salvation, healing, baptism in the Holy Spirit, and the doctrine and government of your church, and all must have signed the Code of Conduct.

Auditions

4. The sanctuary is not the practice room for people to learn to play or sing. No music is better than bad music, so select members after auditioning them and assuring yourself of their musical skills. Remember we are ministers of music, not rock stars. Leaders have to be firm and eliminate grandstanders.

5. Leaders must use love and compassion when sisters or brothers want to be on the music ministry team but cannot carry a tune in a bucket or play miserably. You have to choose between making them sad for a short time till they get over it or making the congregation miserable indefinitely!

6. Musical excellence is the goal we must aspire to. God invented music, and it is to His glory that we sing and play in church. Let us do it with diligence; let us practice and work to be better and better at what we do.

Duties and Responsibilities

7. Faithfulness: Members must show up for all practices and events or have a good reason not to. They should attend regular Bible study and diligent study it at home.

8. Dress code. Since they are on a platform, they should set an example for dress in church. This is always a local option, but women should never wear short skirts or skimpy outfits. No one should dress flamboyantly or in ways that draw attention to himself or herself. The congregation's attention should be on the words of the songs, not the people singing them.

9. They should arrive early for all services and events and have equipment and instruments set up and tuned prior to the arrival of the congregation or other audience. Set-up chores should be done out of the view of the congregation when possible.

10. They should coordinate with the audiovisual ministry so all overhead songs are cued up correctly and all mikes and other electronic equipment are in place and ready.

11. Song selection. Leaders must select songs and review all lyrics to make sure all are appropriate for the church and its beliefs. They should choose songs that uplift people and glorify God; they should choose music that contains scriptures and words with a positive confession of God's Word.

There are no specific job descriptions for the worship team in this manual. The individual job descriptions need to be locally developed by the leader and the team. Specifics such as times of practices, who stands where, who plays background at altar calls, what to do in the absence of a member, and so on are all local concerns. A separate list of general rules and procedures for the music ministry can be drafted using this format as a starting point.

The following two pages contain the job description for the music/worship leader. The job description may give you ideas on how to develop specific job descriptions for each instrumentalist and vocal member of the worship team.

Job Description: Music/Worship Leader
Reports to senior pastor

(This job description came from class notes from the School of Helps Ministry, Faith Christian Fellowship in Tulsa, Oklahoma. It is intended as the basic outline for a final copy you should develop locally.)

Functions

1. Worship leaders lead! They do not get into worship themselves. They must be attentive to the spiritual tone in the service and lead the congregation in worship. Maintain eye contact. When the worship leader gets into personal worship, the congregation is distracted by them. The result is the congregation not getting into worship themselves. The congregation may enjoy it, but their enjoyment is not what a worship service is all about

2. No preaching, testimony, or operettas

3. No vocal or instrumental runs by anyone on the team unless approved by the worship leader.

4. When the leader discerns the yoke is broken and the congregation is ready for the Word, he or she should turn the service over to the pastor or do it at the time decided upon prior to the service.

5. A good musical blowout is good once in a while and will get the congregation emotionally ready and hopefully spiritually ready to receive what God has for them that day, but a big blowout every week is too much.

6. Worship leaders build relationship with the congregation out front with eye contact. Each backup singer sings to a different place in the room so all the congregation gets eye contact at some point.

7. All songs in the same key at a service. Change keys next week, not during a service.

8. All songs must be planned in advance with smooth movement between songs. Pause as the Holy Spirit leads to give time for gifts of the Spirit to move.

9. The congregation's attention should be on praising God, not admiring the showmanship of the music team. They are not performers.

10. The overhead or AV operator must know the flow of the songs so the correct words are on screen every time. Switching around confuses the overhead operator and impedes

the Spirit. When the congregation is confused about what words they should be singing, it takes their attention off worship.

11. Rotate songs frequently so the congregation learns many songs in the year. Old hymns must be included.

12. Praise—fast songs get people emotionally prepared for worship. They should be aimed at the senses. That makes people comfortable and is not threatening to the unsaved. Emotion can be released here. This is when we acknowledge God's acts and greatness. (At this point, people may be self-conscious if others are watching them raise their hands.) Praise is physical in song. Worship is a spiritual connection with God.

13. Worship—usually slower songs that acknowledge who God is. Not as comfortable in the flesh. Here is where you begin to communicate with God. You move out of the realm of emotion into worship. (At this point, people should not care if anyone is looking at them raising their hands!)

14. Worship leaders' job is to ready the ground for the seed of the Word to be sown by the speaker.

15. Worship leaders also must plan for special music. A psalmist is one who sings or plays to the Lord to minister to Him. The congregation watches. This was done in the Old Testament, and when done in our services, it is usually introduced as a solo. In a worship service, it is more correctly a psalmist.

16. Recorded or live music should start fifteen minutes prior to the service so people in the sanctuary quiet down. Visiting should happen outside the sanctuary before and after services.

17. One song leader should control the operation. Directions should be given discreetly and unobtrusively to sound people and musicians with prearranged hand signals.

18. No new songs at services; new songs should be learned and thoroughly rehearsed by the musicians and singers before introducing them to the congregation.

19. Song leader must control the musicians and singers making sure they attend practices and conduct themselves according to directions.

Sample Release Form for Guest Speaker or Music Minister

Name of church
Date, time of services

I understand that (fill in name of church) will make video and audio records of my visit and any music performed for distribution and sale to its members.

By signing below I do / do not (circle one) give the name of church the right to duplicate and sell or give away my likeness, words, and/or music performance to their members.

Both parties agree that if permission is given to sell, no sales or distribution of the media will occur for seventy-two hours after my last engagement at the church to enable me to sell recordings and books during my stay.

Name of Guest speaker or performer _____

Signature _____date_____

Name of pastor _____

Pastor's signature_____ date _____

CHAPTER 12

Electronic Media Ministry

This is a behind-the-scenes but very important ministry that is essential for the smooth operation of a church. It has evolved over the years from maintaining PA systems and perhaps overhead projectors to a full-media operation involving computers, social media, church websites and blogs, video and audio recording, and production of CDs and DVDs

These are the ways by which a church is able to spread the Word to people outside its walls and allow the Word to be passed from person to person without regard to physical limitations. This ministry also provides a product for which people will pay, so it must be of the highest quality. People unable to come to church may rely on the electronic transmission of God's message as their only connection to the church, so we must be diligent about delivering it on time every time.

Detailed, day-to-day processes will be individual for every church. They have differing needs and budgets when it comes to equipment. In this chapter, we will present a structure you can develop to guide your ministry and train new people.

General Instructions

1. All members should have been through the Ministry of Helps Training Program so they have familiarity with salvation, healing, baptism in the Holy Spirit, and the doctrine and government of your church.

2. All members should arrive forty-five minutes early for all services so they can check out and adjust all equipment. Have a checklist next to each piece of equipment so someone can quickly determine if it is set up correctly or needs resetting.

3. Have the instruction manuals close by in the booth at all times for each piece of equipment in case any last-minute problems crop up.

4. Coordinate with the music minister so every song is cued up in the correct order and any specific instructions from the music minister are noted for the operator(s) who will be running the equipment.

5. Dress in normal church clothing, well groomed and clean in body and breath.

6. Accurate, permanent, and complete records should be kept on each piece of equipment, and all equipment should be numbered so over time, the costs for the specific pieces of equipment and their maintenance will be known. This will assist in future purchases

because new people will have a maintenance history and can make better choices on brands, etc. when buying new gear.

7. Members must stay alert during services even when everyone else in the church is having a great time worshiping in the Spirit. When a pastor or minister asks for all eyes closed, it does not mean the media people! They must be alert to raise or lower the volume on a mike, move a TV camera, or do some other job to properly cover the service. Their time to join in is when they are not on the job in the booth or control room.

8. The ministry leaders must rotate themselves and their members so everyone can participate in worship once in a while. Those who have to stay in a booth all the time will eventually burn out, and you will lose them permanently.

Privacy Issues

9. Church legal counsel should be consulted to determine what can and what cannot be duplicated and put on the web or electronic media. Never post a prayer request containing private information about an individual or a situation that should remain confidential. This is another reason that the pastor must have ultimate responsibility and authority as to what is uploaded to any media.

10. Obtain permission in writing from any guest speaker or musical group before recording them. Most speakers and groups have CDs or DVDs for sale. In those cases, you may have to keep the recordings of the service private and not distribute them to your congregation. Have an understanding before any service of what the rules are, and have it in writing. (See sample at the end of this chapter.)

11. Any social-media accounts containing the name of the church must be monitored and controlled by the pastor. No entries or replies to comments should be allowed without the specific permission of the pastor. Social media is very immediate and is out on the web permanently, so anything coming from the local church must always be vetted by the pastor before posting—no exceptions.

12. If you are recording a regular service and the pastor has authorized immediate recording and duplication, have sufficient supplies so you can burn a number of copies quickly and present them to guests or delivered to shut-ins immediately after the service.

Television and Satellite

13. All licenses and FCC permits must be in place and plainly posted. This part of the ministry, like all others, must be operated in strict compliance with all secular laws. We must set the example for the world of integrity in all our operations.

14. Payments of royalties. Use of copyrighted songs in services and duplication in media require payment to the originator.

15. Church music releases can be obtained by subscription at Christian Copyright Licensing International, which can be contacted on the Internet.

16. Two other major organizations do this for the balance of the music business. You may have to have releases from more than one organization, so check your songbook's titles or list of songs you use and make sure the organization you choose represents the writers of those specific songs. The one (or two or three) you choose to use is dependent on the type of music you will be duplicating or playing in your church.

17. Be sure and sign up with the appropriate body, since playing or duplicating copyrighted work without permission is theft and puts you in violation of the eighth commandment.

18. Many times, workers in the electronic ministry will have to be hired outside the church because of the skills and technical expertise needed. Ministry members should be mindful that all these technicians may not be committed Christians; the members should take every opportunity to assist them in coming to Christ when the time is right. Every effort should be made to ensure that all members of the staff are regular tithing members of the local church.

An Admonition to the Church

19. If you want to build engagement to build the body of Christ, keep learning and never stop.

    • Learn who your audience is.
    • Learn what they want to read.
    • Learn where they prefer to converse.
    • Learn how to be open.
    • Learn that you're never 100 percent correct.

20. Who is your audience? The church needs people in the young-family age groups. These people have ideas, are energetic, are better educated, and have jobs that will allow them become involved in church life. Most important, they have children—the next generation of Christians.

21. What do they read? This isn't relevant in a sense; you want to encourage them to read the Bible. But do they read blogs? If so, do you have one? Do they read web pages? If so, do you have one?

22. How do they converse? In many cases, electronically.

23. How is your church open to this age group? Many are not, and many in this age cohort think Christians are next to a "cult." In many cases, we are not involved in the community or have any presence that indicates we are even here.

24. We know we are never 100 percent correct, but we need to communicate that we are here even though we don't have all the answers. We have to let them know that we serve a God who can help people in their times of need because He has the answers.

25. We must realize the penalty for inaction. Many churches are paying for that it in the falling-away of members, financial distress, lack of volunteer workers, and aging church populations.

Solutions

26. Pray, ask God for guidance, and consider the following.

   • A vital and active web presence that includes a church web page, Facebook, and Twitter accounts.
   • A web address mentioned in the church sign out front that includes an invitation: "Join us on Facebook."
   • A 4 x 4 4 Jesus club or some other club you sponsor to attract people to your church for monthly meetings.
   • An organized, concerted effort to restore some of the young people and families who have left churches and are presently unchurched.

CHAPTER 13

Bookstore

A church bookstore has three main functions.

1. To carry and provide a source for the literature the pastor (as shepherd of the flock) knows is biblically based and will edify the congregation. Most of this will likely be locally produced recordings on various media of events at the church. Also, some churches may have items printed and for distribution to the congregation, not the public.

2. To have a convenient location for the purchase of regular Bible bookstore items where there is no Christian bookstore in the area.

3. To carry the books that local bookstores may not because the owners disagree with the teachings presented. You may run across an owner who has strong negative opinions about charismatic gifts or a specific topic or author; this may cause you to carry faith-based books in your inventory.

If a local bookstore carries an item, the church's bookstore might not want to carry it; competing with a local, Christian-owned business is not a good witness. Establishing close relations with local bookstores is a good idea; perhaps you can get ideas for improving your store from them if they know you are not competing with them.

Method of Operation

4. Dress in normal church attire and be clean of body and breath.

5. Arrive early at every service and have the store open before the first people enter. (This and all other hours of operation should be cleared with the pastor.)

6. Order and keep adequate stock of all items for sale. Pastor must approve of any new titles or other merchandise.

7. Mark all items with the proper price. Keep a detailed and accurate inventory and records of sales. Report all sales and turn funds over to the church secretary treasurer or other designated person after each service.

8. Keep the change or petty cash drawer in a safe place, count it each day, and turn over the record of sales and cash or checks retaining only the change fund, whatever amount deemed necessary by the ministry leader and the church secretary-treasurer.

9. The petty cash/change fund should be periodically checked by church staff to make sure all accounting is accurate.

10. Guest ministers may want to use your staff to help them staff their book tables. If so, give all monies to them and do not run any of the sales through the church's accounting system unless previous arrangements have been made to do so.

11. One example is when the church buys books or electronic media from the guest for resale. In this case, the guest is paid in full for the cost of the items and all the proceeds stay with the church.

12. Whether items are sold to the church at discount or at full retail should be discussed in advance. Some churches buy a supply at full price to be a blessing to the guest and later sell them to the congregation at the same price.

13. The bookstore is also in charge of keeping an adequate supply of give-away items for use in the sanctuary, including Bibles for the newly saved and Bible tracts used by the exhorter ministry.

14. Publishing the weekly bulletin is an ancillary duty. It must be done and available to the greeters and church staff prior to any service.

15. It is helpful for each member of the sales staff to read the items in inventory and be able to guide people in purchasing the various books. This is impractical for large bookstores but can work in small churches in which inventories are limited.

16. Your pastor should assist in choosing versions of different Bibles he or she thinks are important for the congregation to study. One of each should be available as a sample for inspection and consideration of purchasers. Some study Bibles are very expensive due to their commentaries and concordances. It's good to have a good study Bible along with inexpensive non-copyrighted King James Versions that can be sold inexpensively and given away by the pastor when someone gets saved.

17. Denominational literature is always a good idea. People should know and appreciate the unique aspects of their church's denomination and be familiar with its teachings.

CHAPTER 14

Hospital and Nursing Home Ministry

This chapter contains two parts—hospital visitation and elder care and nursing home visitation. A job description for a home visitation minister is attached to this chapter.

Hospital visitations have incorrectly been assigned exclusively to the pastor. While the pastor may want to do this often, the burden for praying for the sick is that of the elders: James 5:14 tells us, "Is anyone among you sick? Let him call for the elders of the church, and let them pray over him, anointing him with oil in the name of the Lord." Granted, your pastor is an elder, but the Word is clear—elders plural. The implication is that elders of the church as compared with the leader or pastor of the church should engage in such visitation. The pastor is but one of the elders and should not be expected to make every hospital visit.

General Instructions for Both Ministries

1. They should wear regular church attire and be clean of body and breath.

2. They should be on time to all appointments; have backups if one is ever unable to serve.

3. All members must be regular tithing members of the local church.

4. All must complete the Helps Ministry training and be known to the pastor as Spirit-filled Christians. Members must be able to answer biblical questions and meet and minister to potentially nonbelieving relatives.

5. Members should carry Bibles and tracts and be prepared to minister God's Word correctly and communicate effectively.

6. Whether they are in a hospital, home visitation, or other care facility, they must be mindful of and obedient to whoever is in charge. (Unsaved relatives actually had me escorted out of a hospital by security because I was praying for their relative and they objected to it. This can and does happen. If it does, leave peaceably and with dignity.)

Hospital Visitations

7. A telephone tree should be set up and the name, and contact information for the primary person should appear each week in the bulletin. That person in turn should either make

the visitation or send another elder or the pastor. The pastor should consult with the leader of this ministry and set up procedures to their liking.

8. Gender must be taken into consideration as well as age. Males must pray with males and females with females. Preferably, couples should do all visitations, but this is not always possible.

Confidentiality

9. A written report should be made of all visits and kept in a confidential file by the pastor. No information specific to the illness or injury should ever be disclosed publicly without the permission of the person being prayed for. Their personal privacy is paramount, and it is a violation of federal law to disclose confidential medical information.

10. All of us have witnessed a well-meaning pastor standing in the pulpit asking for prayer for some medical condition or other need. Specific details or specific needs can be unspoken out of respect for the privacy of the person in need. Details are unnecessary and possibly a violation of personal privacy; they should be avoided. The specific condition is no one's business except the person undergoing treatment or having some dire need.

Specifics for Nursing Home and Elder Care Facility Ministry

11. Again, these people must dress appropriate to the facility they visit—normal church clothing and clean of body and breath.

12. Usually, this will be a group with one person leading. They should arrive early. The leader should introduce his or her team to the staff and be guided by their instructions as to where they set up and any time constraints. They should not interfere with meal times or other planned activities at the facility.

13. As is the case with hospital ministers, nursing home ministers should be polite and attentive to owners and staff, who are also candidates for salvation. Nursing home ministers' conduct, demeanor, and polite ministering of God's Word or playing music or other activities are examples to them too.

14. If the nursing home ministers' objective is ministering the Word, they should develop a short program, songs they can participate in (perhaps pass out sheets with the words printed in large letters), a short sermon, a psalm, and a closing song. Some nursing home residents cannot remain attentive for a long time. Leave time for fellowship after the presentation so they have a chance to get to know you and ask questions. Or if possible, you can help them make a decision to follow Christ!

15. Instruments should give way to vocals. Lean toward familiar songs, not contemporary ones the audience might not know. Become familiar with the words so you sing them right every time. Encourage sing-along to get them involved in the program. Some musicians pass out sheets with the words to the songs so the residents can join in.

16. They are ministering in song, *not* performing. Their goal is to bring the love and Word of God to these folks, not put on a show. They should pray before every visit for God's guidance, and they should be as diligent there as they would be at a regular church service.

17. All on the team should pray in the Spirit when they are not doing other things. However, they should do so quietly and discreetly since this could upset those who do not believe in praying in tongues. They are there to minister, not force their Pentecostal or Charismatic views on anyone.

18. Salvation is their primary goal. Baptism in the Holy Spirit and moving in the gifts may or may not follow. They should not compromise the Word. If they discern that the Holy Spirit is calling them to move in the gifts, they should do so. They will be judged by their fruits. If the Holy Spirit called them to do it, things will work out well. If they are doing it on their own authority, it may or may not work out.

19. Someone may request water baptism. The pastor needs to have developed guidelines for the teams in these situations. Some may administer baptism by sprinkling at the facility; it may not be practical because of age or infirmity to take them elsewhere for total immersion. The condition and ability of the person is their primary concern, not a customary way of performing baptisms.

20. They should keep records of names and addresses of all persons who receive individual prayer, baptism, etc. so the pastor can send them a nice letter of congratulations. The leader of this ministry should prepare the letters and get them to the pastor for signature. Sending thank-you letters to the proprietor of the facility is also a good practice.

Position Title: Home Visitation Minister

Accountable to the pastor or pastor's appointed representative

Functions

1. This person or husband-and-wife team coordinates visits to church members at their residences.

2. This is the first point of contact for congregation members to call for home visits for the sick or others who have missed church recently, not the pastor.

3. Each member of this ministry should be provided cards inviting people to your church.

4. Each member should be provided tracts about healing and salvation to be carried in their Bibles if the need for a visit comes up and they are asked to do the visit.

5. No visitation minister who is sick should accept any assignment. This requires having backups on call.

6. Visitation ministers should attempt to find out why those they visit are not attending church regularly and how they could be of help. Perhaps they need transportation, perhaps they feel bad because they cannot tithe, perhaps their mode of dress, and so on.

7. They should be trained to emphasize that the church is the house of God and they should come to church to visit with Him, not to impress other people.

8. They should offer to pray with them. Do they have needs? Can they put a prayer card in the bowl for them for Tuesday evening prayer?

9. They should keep their visits short and not become bothers. They should let those they visit know they are loved and missed.

10. They should report on their visits to the appropriate party in the church.

CHAPTER 15

Jail and Prison Ministry

This ministry is not for the faint of heart or those who are simply curious about what goes on behind bars. It is a place to those called to minister under sometimes rigorous conditions in unpleasant places. Further, they may minister to an audience in which some are attending because it excuses them from something more distasteful than church!

Members of this ministry appreciate the statement "Faith and patience are power twins." It takes a lot of faith and patience to minister effectively in this setting, but the rewards are worth it. Some of the inmates have lost hope. Prison ministers can bring the hope of Christ and an overcoming life with Him to them even though they are incarcerated. Paul was in jail when he wrote many of the books of the Bible!

It takes mature Christians working in the supernatural gifts of wisdom and discernment to be effective. Inmates have been called cons for decades not just because they have been convicted and are now convicts but because they are sometimes good con artists and may try to manipulate the system (and prison ministers) to their advantage. Prison ministers should be wise and protect themselves spiritually as well as physically at all times.

Functions

1. The primary goal is to preach salvation and hope to inmates to let them know that even if loved ones have let them down or shunned them, God loves them.

2. Prison ministers should stick to the Word so faith can be built up in the people they witness to and they can receive all God has for them. Romans 10:17: "So then faith comes by hearing, and hearing by the word of God. Not by our opinions or experiences."

3. All members should have been through the Ministry of Helps Training Program so they have familiarity with salvation, healing, baptism in the Holy Spirit, and the doctrine and government of their local church. They should lead those to whom they minister to discover who they are in God's kingdom.

4. They should have the following scriptures marked in their Bibles and know them thoroughly.

   - Romans 5:8: Christ died for sinners like us.
   - Romans 8:10: Christ is in us.
   - Romans 8:17: We're joint heirs with Jesus.

- 1 Corinthians 2:16: We have the mind of Christ.
- Galatians 4:7: We are no longer slaves but heirs.
- Ephesians 2:10: We were created in His workmanship.
- Ephesians 3:14–21: We should learn the mysteries of His love.
- Philippians 4:13: We can do all things through Christ.
- Philippians 4:19: He will supply all our needs through Christ.

This is a partial list. Pick a favorite that works for you.

5. Prison ministers should teach prisoners that it is not important to God where they are now or how they lived their lives; God's concern is how they will live their lives from now on.

6. They should teach prisoners that as Christians, God gives them the freedom to chart their eternal destinies. He forgives them of sin and welcomes them into eternal life with Him whether they are in prison or free. God's best for all of us will be found by living our lives in a manner that ensures we spend it with Him in eternity regardless of where we live.

7. They should encourage prisoners to get involved in activities that prepare them for life on the outside. They should distribute Bibles if that is permitted.

8. Their goal is to bring the Word of God, not become involved with prisoner rehabilitation. They are there to straighten out their spiritual lives, not be occupational therapists or social workers.

9. They should seek counsel from experienced jail and prison ministers so they learn the ins and outs and don't repeat the mistakes of others. They should work with experienced prison ministers until they are experienced enough to proceed on their own. (Your denomination may have training materials for prison ministry.)

CHAPTER 16

Food, Clothing, and Shelter Ministry

This is another ministry whose leader has to be strong and discerning, not easily conned by greedy people who pretend to be in need. Christians have traditionally been easy marks for con artists who work the system so they do not have to work. We experience visits from alcoholics and narcotics users who prefer to spend their money on booze and drugs and not on food and shelter. (See number 14 below.)

When selecting ministry members, be sure to send all candidates through the Ministry of Helps Training Program so they are familiar with salvation, healing, baptism in the Holy Spirit, and the doctrine and governance of your church.

This ministry requires lifting and physical exertion, so be mindful of that when people ask to join. Usually, distribution times are half days during the week, so folks who work full-time may not be candidates for this ministry.

As Christians, we must always be ready to help those in genuine need. Matthew 10:16 advises us to be wise as serpents and gentle as doves. Our primary mission is to spread the gospel of Jesus Christ, and part of that is helping those in need with God's love and tangible assistance when needed.

Jesus Himself admonished us to feed the poor.

> He also said to him who invited Him, "When you give a dinner or a supper, do not ask your friends, your brothers, your relatives, nor rich neighbors, lest they also invite you back, and you be repaid. But when you give a feast, invite the poor, the maimed, the lame, the blind. And you will be blessed, because they cannot repay you; for you shall be repaid at the resurrection of the just." (Luke 14:12–14)

We help others and store up heavenly blessings for ourselves. Public welfare departments have supplanted the church in this area. Christian churches and ministries must take back this service to the poor and share God's bounty with them while ministering His saving grace.

Functions

1. Coordination with local food banks and supermarkets that donate food is essential to success. Once you start a ministry, people will learn to rely on you, so you have to be steadfast and faithful in delivering services.

2. Get to know the people you are blessing in this program. Find out what else they need and try to point them toward solution to their problems so they will not have to rely on the food and shelter ministry permanently. Have referral resources to battered women's shelters, unwed mothers' services, employment training services, free medical services, drug treatment centers, and other ministries to assist the recipients get back on their feet.

3. Pass out tracts with food, and have Christian literature and Bibles handy to give out.

4. Converts must come to Jesus of their own accord as led by the Spirit. We cannot make salvation or church membership a requirement before we give food or shelter.

Cash

5. A foundational truth for these ministries is "Don't give cash." If someone needs money, say, for fuel, have an agreement with a provider to give the needed service with a voucher that you will pay later. Vouchers should identify the person and the vehicle and be absolutely nontransferable so they cannot be converted into cash.

6. If you suspect or know someone is just freeloading and refuses to find work, advise the pastor and ministry leader and be led by their instructions on how to handle the matter. They have the responsibility to let that person know,

    For even when we were with you, we commanded you this: If anyone will not work, neither shall he eat. For we hear that there are some who walk among you in a disorderly manner, not working at all, but are busybodies. (Thessalonians 3:10–11)

7. We do not want to get into a situation in which ministers argue with or question the need of the person requesting service. We know that lazy people should not get services, but it is the leader's responsibility to prevent abuse. This must be a decision by the leader, not the ministry member, after speaking to the person involved. You do not want to serve freeloaders, but you have to be very careful how you refuse service. Proverbs 12:24 tells us a slothful person will not prosper.

8. Try to identify people who are members of another church. When you find them, the ministry leader should notify you so he or she can coordinate with the other pastor to verify need and determine if they are receiving benefits from that church's ministry too. Some people might be too proud to admit at their churches that they have fallen on hard times or to take from their churches. Their pastors should know the situation so their churches can assist their members directly.

9. If you provide shelter, have some work for the recipients to do so they feel they are making their own way. Work is satisfying and develops the habit of hard work. This is not always possible, but do it if you can.

If the Person in Need Is a Church Member

10. Pastors should determine if those in need were tithing regularly before their needs came up. If not, they should still get benefits, but they should be advised that the tithes of others are providing this help and that when they start making money, they need to stop robbing God and tithe. This sounds harsh, but it is biblical. In my years of ministry, the overwhelming majority of people who ended up needing financial help did not practice tithing!

11. They should tithe out of their need with work and what little resources they have. They need to test God and see if He will help them get on their feet again: "Give, and it will be given to you: good measure, pressed down, shaken together, and running over will be put into your bosom. For with the same measure that you use, it will be measured back to you" (Luke 6: 38).

12. Pray for the member for deliverance from the present temporary situation, thanking God in advance for His answer to your prayer.

13. You do not have start from scratch with this ministry; you can affiliate with major denominations, food banks, the 700 Club, the local Salvation Army, or a church with an established program.

CHAPTER 17

Bible Study and Home Cell Groups

Bible study groups and home cell groups will be covered in one chapter since they are similar in organization. The key differences is that Bible study groups usually have a methodical study of the Bible as their core function, whereas home cell groups may function like home churches or fellowship groups for like-minded people.

I have been in churches in which men's fellowship groups went fishing, camping, or hunting or played golf. They invited non-churchgoers to come, and they used these outings to evangelize the unsaved by just fellowshipping with them and having a good time. Many people think Christians are stuffy and don't know how to have fun, but over time, many become saved and join the church.

Leadership Selection

Pastors must carefully pick leaders. These individuals (and couples) serve like mini-pastors ministering to the needs of those in their care. Formal training programs may be used by pastors to fully equip ministers in these roles.

The pastor must be very clear about the role of these folks and be sure of their spiritual walks and that they are mature and able to lead effectively as representatives of God and the local church.

Our leaders must be equipped to lead people in Bible study without wrangling about every tiny detail.

> Remind them of these things, charging them before the Lord not to strive about words to no profit, to the ruin of the hearers. Be diligent to present yourself approved to God, a worker who does not need to be ashamed, rightly dividing the word of truth. (2 Timothy 2:14–15)

Picking people to lead ministry is a serious role for pastors and others who make these selections, so they must be done with care. Resist the temptation to just plug someone in to fill a vacancy. Not having a class is better than a bad class or one led by an unqualified leader.

Functions of Bible Study and Home Cell Leaders

1. All leaders of the groups should be regular tithing members of the local church.

2. All should have been through the Ministry of Helps Training Program so they are familiar with salvation, healing, baptism in the Holy Spirit, and the doctrine and governance of your church.

The Groups' Operation

3. If the Bible studies or home groups are structured, the pastor must choose the format and the content and make sure all groups conform to the format so the same thing is taught in each home group or Bible study.

4. If the leaders are free to guide their own study, they must inform the pastor in writing of the topics and an outline of what they are teaching.

5. The objectives and methods of operation must be clearly stated in writing and agreed to by the local church leadership and the ministry leaders.

6. There should be formats and reporting methods that are clear and adhered to by the home group or Bible study leader.

7. The pastor and the local church are ultimately responsible for these ministries held under their legal umbrella, so they must be kept appraised of what is going on since they can be held legally liable for any malfeasance or improper behavior.

8. The pastor or an associate or assistant should periodically drop in on scheduled meetings and observe what goes on. It shows the participants that the local church is interested in them and their welfare. It is not a matter of mistrusting the leader; it is supporting their leadership by showing up and participating in their meetings.

Schedules

9. Meetings of both types of groups should be regularly scheduled and the time and place given publicity in the church weekly bulletin or bulletin board and absolutely on the church's website.

10. Meetings should be held without fail; a new visitor could show up and discover a meeting has been canceled. That person might think the group is disorganized and not show up again. You must be a good witness and be faithful in having meetings when scheduled. Have a backup so even if the leader is unable to attend, the meeting will take place on schedule.

11. Going overtime. This is a big no-no. Stop the meeting on time and release those who want or have to leave. Some may want to stay and fellowship; this depends on where the meeting is held. Some may have to get up early to work, and it would be an undue burden for them to stay late. Be sensitive to the person who is offering his or her home for the meeting by keeping to the schedule. We need to be good stewards of people's time.

Meeting Format

12. The group leader sets the pace.

13. Welcome everyone and introduce everyone every time. Then when a visitor shows up, such introductions will be a normal part of the format.

14. Open in prayer; ask God's blessings on the meeting or the outing. If you are traveling, pray God's traveling mercies on all the cars or other means of transportation.

15. Start and stop on time every time!

16. If the group is for fellowship, the activity or visiting can start. Once folks finish their refreshments, the leader can share a short (five to ten minutes or so) teaching and then answer questions. Then you can resume fellowship and close in prayer and dismiss.

17. If it is an outing, the dismissal may happen in a parking lot. Remember to leave on time and to do your best to get everyone home when the outing is scheduled to be over. If you go to a ball game or concert, you may be governed by the schedule of the event.

18. If you are conducting a serious, "real" Bible study, the participants should decide on the format. Will you have discussion? Will the others just listen? The time limits, etc., should all be known by everyone and start and stop on time.

19. Remember the primary reason for any event is Christian fellowship that uplifts members and shows nonbelievers we are fun to be with. It is fellowship and evangelism rolled into one.

20. The ministry leader should consistently inform group leaders and Bible study leaders to invite unchurched people, not members of other congregations. We are ambassadors for Christ to bring people to a saving knowledge of Him, not proselytizing people from other churches. It's fine to invite other Christians to fellowship outings but not for the purpose of getting them to switch churches.

21. Leaders should be in a constant search for new leaders from their group members. The best-case scenario is that your group grows too big because of new converts and needs to split. In these cases, a new leader from within the group will already have a relationship with some of the members.

22. New leaders should be picked early on so they can attend the required training programs and be ready when their time comes. Meanwhile, they can be backup for the regular leader.

Tips for Group Leaders

23. Listen to your members and try to help them through rough spots in life. However, you are not a pastor or counselor, so be aware of your qualifications and limitations. Refer those in need to professionals or the pastor for help in serious situations.

24. Remember 1 Corinthians 1:10—everyone should be of one accord, no gossip or backbiting, no criticism of the pastor or the church. Keep the discussions positive. Your role is to create and maintain a positive, uplifting group that makes everyone comfortable.

25. Be responsible for follow-up with guests; invite them back and minister to their spiritual needs.

26. Home groups sometimes hold potlucks or other gatherings and invite neighbors of the home where the meeting is taking place. Just be nice; let them enjoy the fellowship, but don't preach to them. Let them experience a time of fun with Christians with no pressure to join the church. This serves to perhaps thank them for taking up all the parking spots on the block once a week! Maybe they will be less annoyed.

Position Title: Home Group Leader

Accountable to the pastor or local leader for home groups and follow-up

Functions

1. They conduct home Bible studies at their homes or at host residences.

2. Home group leaders must nominate an alternate and have that person or couple approved by the associate pastor for home groups.

3. They should hold regularly scheduled meetings using a format approved by the associate pastor for home groups. Fellowship time and refreshments should be a part of every meeting.

4. Bible studies should be simple enough that if unsaved people attend, they will not be confused with technical details. When they have visitors, they should switch to simple topics such as salvation, healing, forgiveness, love, caring for others, or prayer for loved ones. Complex topics should be discussed when everyone is at about the same level.

5. They may want the group to read the Bible or one book of the Bible and have members comment. Have members read footnotes or concordances to teach people how to search the scriptures and to study to show themselves approved by God.

6. They should keep it short and fun and not let any one person dominate the meeting.

7. They should encourage all attendees to talk and determine where they are spiritually rather than deliver a sermon.

8. Prayer time with prayer requests taken is essential. People must see their leaders praying and be encouraged to pray. The answers come from God, not from us.

CHAPTER 18

Bus and Transportation Ministry

This is a valuable but expensive outreach for a local church. Purchasing and maintaining passenger vehicles is expensive and time consuming. Recruiting and training drivers (and backups) who may be required to have specialized driver's licenses is also a challenge. But if your church's vision is outreach to nearby areas or you have traveling musicians or groups, this may be an option for you.

Leadership must have experience in coordinating transportation and arranging for vehicle maintenance if owned vehicles are used.

Drivers

1. All drivers must have completed the Ministry of Helps Training Program and be comfortable witnessing Christ to others.

2. All drivers carrying children must have police background checks on file.

3. All drivers must have the applicable drivers' licenses for the types of vehicles driven.

4. All drivers must have current motor vehicle department records of citations and accidents on file at the church and updated annually. Ministry leaders must monitor this and prohibit drivers from driving unless their records are updated and on file.

5. Drivers must use trip reports for each trip (see below).

6. One ticket or accident may be acceptable. However, your insurance carrier may have different requirements.

7. Any drug or alcohol violation is disqualifying.

8. Your driver selection and training should mirror that of the local school system.

9. These stringent requirements are for safety but also so we "avoid the appearance of evil" by allowing an unqualified person to drive on our behalf. The Old King James Bible says in 1 Thessalonians 5:22, "Abstain from all appearance of evil." The word *appearance* in Greek means any fashion, shape, or sight of evil. If we let people drive just for our

convenience or to please them but they aren't qualified, that is the appearance of evil, and the secular press and lawyers would have an easy time making our church look bad.

10. The ministry leader must have sufficient qualified backup drivers to handle trips when someone is unable to handle a scheduled drive.

11. Drivers must be very polite and courteous when driving in God's service. They have to set an example of Jesus's peace and love when driving as well as when they're not.

12. If it is possible and legal to have your drivers attend local school bus training classes, that would be preferable to inventing in one of your own. There may be commercial driving schools that can provide this service too. Again, another expense that the church would have to bear. This is not an inexpensive ministry!

Scheduling

13. Have definite schedules for regular trips with specific pickup and drop-off points unless you are going to and from individual households.

14. Have sign-up sheets for specific requests that list time, dates, number of passengers, destinations, any overnight stays, and other information to assist the leader in scheduling the trip.

15. Have lead-time rules to prevent last-minute trips that could make it difficult to find a driver on the spur of the moment.

General Guidelines

16. You need to have an "anti-bumping" policy. If people who have not signed up for a trip show up, they can go space permitting—no playing favorites.

17. When private cars are used on official trips of the church (as opposed to giving someone a ride), leaders must make sure that the owner's insurance protection is at least as high as the church's. Your insurance professional can guide you in this matter.

18. Vehicles should not be loaned out to congregation members for private use; only official trips for church activities should be allowed.

19. All vehicle use should be controlled by the ministry leader, and that person is responsible for all maintenance and use of every vehicle.

Vehicle Appearance

20. Spend money on high-quality paint jobs and professional lettering so you can project a positive and professional image of God's church. Shabby, dirty, and unkempt buses send a poor message to the unsaved.

21. A dirty or shabby vehicle gives the impression that it is also poorly maintained and may prevent parents from letting their kids ride in them.

22. A clean, comfortable, and well-maintained bus attracts riders to commercial buses; it follows that clean and tidy buses will attract people to ride those that God owns!

Maintenance and Inspection

23. Have a regular maintenance and inspection program. Many jurisdictions have school bus inspection and maintenance inspection guidelines in law or regulation form. These should be adopted and followed diligently by the bus ministry. Each vehicle must have a file (or electronic file) that has its complete maintenance and inspection record for the entire time you own it.

24. Have printed pre- and post-trip inspection and cleanliness checklists for the drivers and require their use on all trips. Keep them on file or scan them in electronic files for each vehicle. In the event of an accident, you will want to prove your church has been diligent about vehicle safety. Computer programs for recordkeeping of bus operations are commercially available.

25. Dozens of sample bus inspection reports are on the Internet. Pick one and require it to be used for every trip, and keep them or digitize and save them.

CHAPTER 19

Premises Maintenance

How a church looks inside and out positively or negatively impresses visitors. It will have a lot to do with whether they come in or stay after a visit. Carnal people are concerned with what things look like, and the first impression you make will be judged by their carnal minds, not their spiritual concerns. Pastors have known for years that moving a new soul from a carnal to a spiritual way of viewing the world is a slow process.

If your facility is not clean and comfortable, you may never have the chance to minister to their spiritual needs. They won't stay around long enough for you to have any positive affect on them.

Eliminate Distractions

1. Whatever part of your facility they visit should point toward Christ. Trash or dirty restrooms are distractions that make them forget the sermon.

2. Use pastel or other light-color paints so the place looks bright and airy. Display pictures of biblical topics and pleasant decor.

3. Air conditioning and heating should be in good repair so there is no temperature discomfort to get their minds off the Word.

4. Lighting inside and out should make people feel secure. This is very important in certain areas when the church is in a less-than-secure area.

Parking

5. Keep parking lots and areas clean and tidy. Have staff and workers park in outer areas to keep close spots open for visitors.

6. Have legally mandated handicapped parking clearly delineated with the proper signage.

Building maintenance is the responsibility of the ministry leader who in some cases may need to hire a facility manager to handle a larger church. In this chapter, wherever ministry leader is mentioned, you may instead use the term *facility manager*. Ideally, the facility manager will be a church member and leader and function as both. If you have both, one of them has to have the last word and be ultimately responsible for this ministry and the facility. (A suggested job description for a facilities manager is at the end of this chapter.)

The ministry leader is responsible for knowing the amount in the building fund and any maintenance fund and staying within the written guidelines for expenditures. The leader must coordinate with the church board or secretary treasurer when repairs exceed a specific amount.

Another important responsibility is to obtain bids from vendors for repairs that cannot be done by members or church volunteers. The leader has to supervise these repairs whether done by volunteers or outside vendors. The leader should not authorize payment by the church secretary treasurer until he or she is confident the repairs were done correctly and to specification.

Work Orders

7. Design a work order (or purchase order) that specifies the work to be done. It should include a detailed list of the entire job, who will do it, how much it will cost, and the reason for doing it. This should be approved by the pastor or church leadership before the ministry leader initiates the job.

8. When the work is complete, the ministry leader will sign off on it and forward it to the appropriate church office along with the final cost. It should be filed appropriately with facility maintenance records. These records are essential so that the end-of-year financial statement to the congregation has an accurate figure for the money spent on facility maintenance. If someone wants a detailed list of repairs, the information should be immediately available.

9. The ministry leader should familiarize himself or herself with the congregation and solicit help from tradespeople who might be able to volunteer their time and effort.

10. Facility managers should familiarize themselves with reliable, Christian-owned businesses and give preference to those businesses whenever possible. Acts 6:3 admonishes us to choose Spirit-filled people from among us (Christians) that we can appoint over the manual tasks that need to be done (my wording).

11. Be loyal to the contractors who work for you. Bidding out for the cheapest price is okay, but it does not build a sense of loyalty. In the event of an emergency repair at an odd hour, the contractor or tradesman you have been loyal to all along will be more apt to help you than one chosen randomly out of the phone book or that had a low price on one or another job.

Janitorial

12. This is an ongoing duty. Repairs and heavy maintenance occur less frequently. You should have a church member hired to do this and make sure facilities are cleaned after every use. In a large church, it may be more efficient to hire a maintenance company to care for the facilities.

13. Restrooms are a priority as are the nursery and children's areas. These are the first two places moms and dads will notice, and if they find deficiencies, they may not come back! Keep the facility clean and tidy at all times. Have disinfectant wipes or soaps in all classrooms and restrooms, and have signs suggesting everyone use them.

14. If space permits, have baby-changing stations in restrooms.

15. The ministry leader should coordinate with the youth pastor and see if the teens can help the regular crew in cleanup after services. This can be their way of tithing if they have little or no money.

Security System

This ministry is responsible for purchasing and having installed alarms and security cameras. The ministry leader, facility manager, or pastor (your choice) should be the point person to handle first calls on alarms.

In some jurisdictions, false alarms can incur a cost from local law enforcement. So care, maintenance, and proper use of the alarm system is very important.

Members and staff with alarm codes should be trained on the proper setting and resetting of the alarm. The codes should never be given out to anyone not on a list signed by the pastor. Codes should be assigned only to people with key access to the building, which should be a very limited number of people. Codes must be changed every time anyone cycles out of leadership.

Some old-time members may feel they have a right to a key and the security code. Avoid the temptation to grant that; if you do, they *will* brag about it to someone who does not have such access, and you may end up with a jealousy problem on your hands. Keys to the church and security codes are to be granted on a need, not a favoritism basis.

Position Title: Facility Upkeep Manager
Accountable to (note the immediate supervisor's position/title)

This may entail part time paid individuals. All agreements for pay must be preapproved by the (insert name of the person responsible for contracts) and the senior pastor.

Functions

1. church cleaning after every service

2. landscape maintenance

3. parking lot maintenance—striping, safety, cleanup, etc.

4. obtaining permits and supervising major and minor building projects

5. workday organization and supervision; arranging for contractors when needed; getting youth and adult help for less-technical projects

6. premises security including alarms and cameras

7. other duties regarding the physical church as needed

CHAPTER 20

Office, Computers, Bulletins

Office workers serve essentials function in the local body. There needs to be place where all information and records necessary to operate the church are organized and kept secure.

The members of the church have a right to know that the church's resources are being used and accounted for in a way that complies with standard accounting methods and the bylaws of the church.

Confidentiality

There are legal ramifications for disclosure of confidential records of members. Churches may have names, contact information, financial (giving) information, records of church boards that discuss confidential topics, and other information that if disclosed to unauthorized persons could possibly be illegal, embarrassing, and detrimental to the members involved.

Paper records should be under lock and key; access to them should be controlled and granted only to authorized personnel. Computer records should be password protected; backups of these computer records should be kept offsite.

Let your accounting professional or denominational guidelines guide you about securing all financial records—how long they should be kept, when they can be deleted or shredded, and so on.

Any record containing a meeting for which pastoral confidentiality applies should be filed or stored where only the pastor has access, never in a member's regular file.

Minutes of board meetings at which topics of a confidential nature were discussed such as employee discipline, issues with discipline in the church, or other confidential topics should not be available for members' view.

Other meeting minutes for the various ministries and the normal board meetings should be posted on the bulletin board so all church members can be aware of the discussions regarding church business.

Duties of Office Personnel

In a small church, perhaps only one person will handle all clerical and administrative duties. Clear and detailed job descriptions need to be written for one or more people.

Employees should be evaluated and rewarded or retrained to ensure compliance and completion of their assigned job duties. Employees must have a clear picture of what is required of them, a definition of a job well done, and a guide to how they need to conduct themselves. This is good for the church as the employer and for the employee(s). Everyone is on the same page as to what is expected.

All employees must complete the Ministry of Helps Training Program so they have familiarity with salvation, healing, baptism in the Holy Spirit, and the doctrine and governance of your church. Those on staff should be able to minister God's blessings to those in need just like any Helps Ministry worker.

General Instructions

These should be divided by job description as necessary. These guides are for the office workers or others responsible for church administration whether paid or not.

1. All bills should be paid on time every time. We need to be a good witness to our vendors. We operate on faith while they operate on cash.

2. All correspondence should be handled in a neat and professional manner.

3. All stationery, purchase orders, envelopes, and such should be printed professionally or skillfully handled internally. Our correspondence should glorify God, not make people think He is second rate!

4. All bookkeeping and accounting should be done in a legal and professional manner. Your CPA or other accounting professional or your denomination can advise you about a proper church accounting system to keep your books and store your financial records.

5. Use the accounting system to pay bills and keep your finances up to date daily.

6. Have periodic audits done by your CPA, the denomination, or an internal audit committee. It is important to properly allocate contributions to the various ministries for specified gifts and to keep all accounting data accurate.

7. You should be able to print a detailed interim financial statement on any day of the year that reflects your finances in all areas of the church as of that day. If you diligently keep your computer or paper books, it is a simple report to print (interim, but accurate to that day).

8. It is unprofessional to be unable to report the financial data of the church to members or other authorized people in the denomination on a moment's notice. It is easily accomplished by strict use of an accounting system, and they are not expensive.

9. Our accounting must be above reproach. We must be as accurate as a bank or other financial institution. We are stewards of God's money and answerable to Him and to any civil authority for improprieties. We must glorify God in our practices and be good, faithful stewards for our members.

10. Failure to keep accurate records and accounting brings disgrace on the individual, the pastor, and God. The church ends up looking like a shady business. The world is looking for ways to criticize Christian churches. Our failures in finance get more publicity than if a small business committed the same error or violation.

Computerized Filing

11. Membership lists should be available to the membership and should be published as needed and distributed to the members so they can easily contact each other. If members agree, you could publish your list on the web with passwords so only enrolled members have access.

12. Members should fill out a sheet indicating what personal data they are willing to have published on the list. The church staff may disclose only that information. Some people may not want their emails or phone numbers published; that should be respected.

13. Keep all records of church maintenance, building programs, etc. indefinitely. This is easy with scanning and digitizing records. They can be digitally stored without taking up valuable storage or file space.

14. Purchase and diligently use antivirus and other security software in church computers and on all cell phones used for church business.

Correspondence with Visitors

15. Guest/visitor follow-up letters should be typed from the contact data submitted by the hosts, greeters, and ushers. These letters should be prepared for the pastor's signature each Monday morning or the day after the person visited so they can be mailed as soon as the pastor signs them.

16. Follow-up letters are important tools to document people's visits and make them feel welcome and inclined to visit again.

17. When we show that we care and are diligent in something as small as a follow-up letter, visitors and guests can correctly infer that we will be diligent in other areas of the church. Luke 16:10 tells us, "He who is faithful in what is least is faithful also in much; and he who is unjust in what is least is unjust also in much." Every guest may not know Luke 16:10, but it is common sense, and people will notice.

18. The office staff must send a copy of the letter to the home group or Bible study leader nearest to the residence of the visitor so that ministry leader can also follow up with an invitation to visit a home group or Bible study.

19. If the person has specific need—single parent, college student, youth, senior, or family with young children—the office staff might send the follow-up to a leader better equipped to minister to the new visitor.

20. Send congratulation letter to anyone who has been saved whether he or she received a Bible or not.

21. As people are healed, send appropriate letters encouraging them to read the Bible, study 1 Peter 2:24 and Isaiah 53:5, and hold onto their healing as it was from God and they are worthy to receive it because of Jesus's sacrifice, not how good they are.

22. Encourage those who are baptized in the Holy Spirit to read 1 Corinthians 12–14. Suggest joining a Bible study or home group to help them build their faith. Send a copy of the letter to the appropriate group leader.

23. If any of the people are not regular voting members of the church, have a letter prepared for the pastor's signature inviting them to the next new members' class. Enclose a church brochure if you have one.

24. Compile birthday lists from membership lists and send birthday greetings. Various vendors can sell birthday and anniversary cards that can be imprinted with the church's information. The pastor should sign these on one day of the week, and they can be sent weekly.

Budgeting and Planning Instructions

25. Use the prior year's expenses to sketch out a budget for the new year. Were there recurring expenses such as mortgages, utilities, etc.? These should be categorized and accounts set up to track expenses for each line item.

26. Solicit budget needs from each of the ministry leaders. Sunday school supplies, building maintenance items, etc. are the responsibility of the leaders, who should submit their budget needs at least thirty days before the budget committee meeting.

27. The church business board and pastor must go over each line item and determine if it is reasonable as is or should be changed to better allocate resources. This group must pray prior to their deliberations and invite the Holy Spirit to guide their discussions and decisions.

28. Future expenditures should be anticipated and funds saved to cover these occasional but possibly expensive items. Examples include replacing a roof, repaving a parking lot, constructing a building, or additions for the future. These high-cost items have to be discussed and specific accounts set up to save for those inevitable major expenses.

29. Once this budget is decided upon, it's good business to have all ministry leaders review it. They may have additions or corrections that should go in before you reveal it to the membership.

30. Once the budget is approved, it must be adhered to, and the financial situation of the church must be available upon request to any regular voting member. It is essential that church finances be open and candid so people who may be hesitant to give for fear of bad stewardship will become confident that the church is managing the money properly and legally.

31. Have a small discretionary fund for the pastor so he or she can confidentially assist someone in need. Monies provided from this fund must be reported to the church board in confidential session only and kept confidential. The church members must know that any gifts bestowed by the pastor will be checked by someone else in confidence so the members can be assured that the pastor is not misusing funds.

Various Types of Expenditures

32. Capital expenses: New-building projects, expensive equipment, and the like are major items that last many years. Give long and diligent consideration to all options before deciding on a project. Mistakes can last many years and be very costly.

33. Equipment replacement items: Some equipment has a finite service life. You must budget for replacements as soon as you buy one of these items. Computers, vehicles, and most electronic items fall in this category.

34. Recurring expenses: utilities, mortgages, regular building maintenance, small tools and equipment, and janitorial supplies fall into this category.

35. Your tax professional or your denomination may have or help you develop a list of accounts so they don't get lumped into a "miscellaneous" account. Accounting professionals recommend that only a tiny percentage of expenditures end up labeled in that manner. Be diligent in accounting properly for every penny of God's money.

36. Church accounting software is available commercially; purchase one for the church and use it diligently.

37. Staff salaries and benefits. These must be decided upon by the group given this responsibility by your church bylaws. They may or may not be confidential per your church's bylaws. All salaries and benefits should be in one classification on the financial statement prepared for the congregation. A more-complete and detailed financial statement should be made available to the leaders of the church and to the denomination.

Some official group must go over every tiny item so it can be analyzed and either added to or eliminated from the next budget.

38. Meetings of this salary and benefits setting group should be kept private and should be attended by your tax professional or denominational representative to ensure that salaries and benefits are in line with local norms and are realistic given the income of the church. A bank or lending institution would require this information to make sure you are not overpaying staff.

39. The compensation packages mentioned above should include housing allowances and all other amounts paid to staff. Unless the bylaws require disclosure, salaries and benefits are private matters between the staff member and pastor and the church board.

Office Procedure Manual

40. This is sometimes called the SOP (standard operating procedures) in the military and business worlds but is called the Ministry of Helps manual in this book. They are interchangeable terms for that written standard by which your church's business is conducted.

41. You may use the topics and suggestions in this chapter and indeed the entire manual to develop a locally produced procedures manual for your church. This manual is a good starting point. However, local issues will dictate changes to agree with your bylaws and the preferences of your church leadership and perhaps denominational rules.

42. Attached to many chapters of this manual are job descriptions for some of the ministry leaders. You should have detailed job descriptions of every position and job in the church. This way, aspiring candidates can learn exactly what is expected of them for any job. Also, supervisors will have a standard to judge the performance of the person occupying that job.

43. The SOP should be a public document available to the membership. We must be transparent in the operation of the church to earn the confidence of members and potential members.

44. Attached to this chapter are money counting rules and a sample job description for the church secretary treasurer.

Position Title: Office Staff or Church Secretary Treasurer
Reports to the senior pastor

Functions
(pursuant to your bylaw provisions for this position)

Qualifications

1. be a regular tithing member of this church

2. be proficient with computers and your chosen accounting software

3. have accurate accounting skills, clerical skills, and experience

4. be able to interact effectively with office and community personnel

Responsibilities

5. serves as an officer of the church and is a member of the advisory committee with full voting rights (if that is provided for in your bylaws)

6. maintains church communications including keeping minutes of annual, regular, and special meetings

7. is entrusted with the finances of the church (see details below). Deposits all funds, writes checks (which must be countersigned by the pastor or in an emergency a senior member of the advisory board). Keeps the books with proper itemized accounts of receipts and disbursements.

Annually

8. produces and distributes annual income and expense reports covering all operations and departments of the church

9. produces, files, and distributes appropriate end-of-year tax forms

10. produces, files, and distributes year-end contribution reports by January 31

11. researches and solicits from leaders the data needed for church budget matters

12. purges files as warranted

13. stores all permanent records including membership records from the previous year in a clearly identified, easily retrievable manner

14. maintains accounts payable receipts and individual contribution records in clearly identified, disposable containers for seven years

15. ensures that designated funds are always handled properly and only for the purpose designated. (In the event that funds donated to the church for a purpose that has not been officially designated and a fund established in the financial records, one of two processes can be used: first, the donation can be immediately returned because the reason designated does not fit your church's vision or goals. Second, if the pastor and advisory committee agree, a new account can be established and those funds deposited in it.)

Quarterly

16. computes and processes employee taxes unless a contractor has been hired to do so

"Tell us, therefore, what do You think? Is it lawful to pay taxes to Caesar, or not?" But Jesus perceived their wickedness, and said, "Why do you test Me, you hypocrites? Show Me the tax money." So they brought Him a denarius. And He said to them, "Whose image and inscription is this?" They said to Him, Caesar's." And He said to them, "Render therefore to Caesar the things that are Caesar's, and to God the things that are God's." (Matthew 22:17–21)

(We need to "render unto Caesar" on time every time. Failure to pay payroll taxes is a violation of law and an embarrassment to God's church.)

Monthly

17. reconciles church accounts for monthly board meeting

18. reconciles checkbook balances with bank statements

19. prepares monthly financial reports for board meetings

20. issues and mails payment of mission commitments

21. deposits and submits monthly payroll taxes and forms

Weekly

22. counts, records, and deposits offerings and cash received into the bank (Two or more should be responsible for counting offerings, and the deposit slips in duplicate must be made out at the time of the count and signed by the counters. One copy goes to a member of the church board for later audit use. The Offering Counting Form at the end of this chapter must be used in all cases.)

23. records all individual contributions

24. issues and distributes payroll checks (Payroll checks and any reimbursement checks issued to the person writing the checks must be countersigned. Two signatures are required for all payroll checks unless a paid service is contracted to do so.)

25. deposits quarterly tax-withholding funds in a savings account.

26. processes accounts payable invoices; issues and mails checks as funds permit (Attached a purchase order to all expense checks so a proper audit trail is maintained.)

27. reconciles petty cash receipts with cash on hand

Daily

28. processes incoming calls on bookkeeping matters

29. processes financial mail, invoices, statements, etc.

30. processes purchase orders for office and church supplies. (Every purchase must be supported by a purchase order that is filed with the canceled check for an audit trail.)

31. processes financial transfers and adjustments

32. processes check requisitions as appropriate using purchase order forms

33. maintains an up-to-date record of remaining funds for each department or designated project

34. maintains all financial files in a neat and orderly fashion

35. keeps the pastor apprised of all pertinent financial information including events, activities, problems, and changes

36. carries out the directives of the pastor and board

Online resources are available for all these functions; buy and use an accounting package, and make sure you have specific procedures implemented to ensure honest and transparent evidence of good stewardship of God's resources.

Offering Counting Form

(your church name)

Date _____

Event or Service (AM, PM, midweek, etc.) _____

Pennies	_____ @ $0.01	_____
Nickels	_____ @ $0.05	_____
Dimes	_____ @ $0.10	_____
Quarters	_____ @ $0.25	_____
1/2 dollars	_____ @ $0.50	_____
1 dollars	_____ @ $1.00	_____
	Total coins	$ _____

Ones	_____ $1	_____
Twos	_____ $2	_____
Fives	_____ $5	_____
Tens	_____ $10	_____
Twenties	_____ $20	_____
Fifties	_____ $50	_____
Hundreds	_____ $100	_____

Total currency $ _____

Total number of checks _____ Total amount of those checks $ _____

Total Offering $ _____

Counter _____

Counter _____

Counter _____

Three copies: one with deposit, one to pastor, one to church secretary treasurer

CHAPTER 21

Altar Ministry and Flower Guild

1. This is a ministry for people with limited time to participate in the church's volunteer ministry programs.

2. Providing flowers and other decorations for regular services and delivery of flowers to people in hospitals is the primary activity for this ministry.

3. Members with flower gardens can provide this ministry with little trouble.

4. Purchasing flowers is an option when church funds provide for this.

   • Some flowers may have pollen that irritates some people. Some churches use artificial flowers and plants, and this ministry maintains them by periodic rotation and cleaning.

   • If you use a florist, open an account with that florist and stick with it. Have strict rules as to who can use the account to prevent abuse. Pay the bill on time every week.

5. In a small congregation, this duty may be taken by the host and hostess or the janitorial staff.

6. This ministry also assists the host and hostess ministry in decorating for holidays, pageants, and other special occasions.

CHAPTER 22

Street Ministry

1. In Luke 9:1–6, Jesus sent out His first street ministers. This is also in Mark 16:15–18. The disciples went out two by two and prayed for people, laid hands on the sick, and cast out demons. We each do this in our own way for people we know and meet.

2. Members of organized street ministries go to the next step and train and prepare themselves for witnessing on a larger scale over a period of time.

    *   The keys are training and preparation, having a plan and executing it in a specific way with the objective of brining salvation to larger numbers of people in a public setting.

    *   Training for these efforts can be obtained from denominational sources.

3. Christ-based literature, tracts, etc. should be in ample supply so you can give everyone you meet something for them to remember your conversation.

    *   Find out if the person had a previous church affiliation. If so, encourage him or her to get back in touch with that church and begin fellowship with like-minded Christians.

    *   If they are unaffiliated, invite them to your church. Get their contact information if they are willing to provide it. Follow up with an invitation to your church, and advise them of some of the ministries you provide that might be of interest to them.

4. Prayer

    *   Leaders must lead in prayer prior to embarking on a trip into the field. Members must be "prayed up" with spiritual fuel just as you need to fill a vehicle with fuel before going on a trip. This is serious business, and you are going into the devil's realm to witness; you need to be ready spiritually for his inevitable resistance.

    *   Request permission before praying for anyone. In 1 Timothy 5:22, we read, "Do not lay hands on anyone hastily, nor share in other people's sins; keep yourself pure." The Bible says to not lay hands on someone suddenly. By implication this means touching and praying for them without their permission.

- Before praying, find out what they want you to pray for. Is it healing or just relief from pain? Do they want the ability to cope with a situation or for God to change the situation? Are their requests biblical? Don't just jump in and start praying without a clear objective. People want answers to prayer; find out what the answer is they are seeking, and then pray.

5. Know what resources are available in the community so you can refer people to the place where their needs can be addressed such as

   - food pantries
   - drug and alcohol rehabilitation facilities
   - shelters for battered women and the homeless
   - aid for pregnant, unmarried girls
   - rescue missions in your area

6. Be sensitive to the leading of the Spirit. Another saint may have planted a seed, and you are to water that seed and perhaps not see the harvest.

   - Just do what you can. Leave the long speeches to the politicians; give the loving Word of God in simple terms.

   - Be nice, be available, and don't argue scripture. If Christians from another denomination want to nitpick the fine points of the Word, lovingly inform them that you would be glad to discuss it in another setting. Ask them, "Could we meet at another place and look up our differences and let the Bible tell us which is correct?" Remember the nonbiblical admonition: "A man convinced against his will is of the same opinion still."

   - Have good things to say about other churches and ministries. Remember Jesus' teaching in Luke 9:49–50. As long as they are not against Jesus and preach His message, Jesus says they are okay in His book; they are therefore okay in our book. Street witnessing is about loving Jesus and bringing His love to a lost and dying world, not debating scripture.

7. Dress code

   - Appropriate for the audience. You want to avoid overdressing with expensive clothing or jewelry that calls attention to you and detracts from the message you are bringing.

   - The opposite also applies—being untidy, unwashed, or too informal in dress can detract from the message even if your audience may be homeless and not well groomed. In these situations, you are the example, but still, don't overdress.

CHAPTER 23

How to Create a Ministry Outline

1. When a member of the church approaches the pastor with a desire to start a ministry, he or she should receive a copy of this chapter and a copy of the chapter pertaining to the type of ministry he or she wants to create (if one has not already been created).

    •   Part of the testing of new potential ministry leaders is to determine if they are capable of organizing a ministry and willing to put in the work necessary to get it into operation and sustain it.

    •   The potential new leader should first go to the Ministry of Helps Training class. The Teacher's Guide for conducting this class is an addendum to this manual. (Student manuals are available to purchase in lots of five copies from WestBow, the publisher of this manual.)

2. Pastors can become comfortable that such people are capable of leadership when they bring completed ministry outlines (details below) and provide the names of the people they have lined up to be workers under their leadership in that ministry.

    •   The pastor needs to know who the leader has chosen as the backup person(s). Who will be in control if the leader becomes unable to function in that position? Without a leader, the ministry will fail, so a trained backup is necessary.

    •   If the potential workers have not attended the Ministry of Helps Training Program, a good idea is to have them all train at the same time and add a week to go over items specific to this new ministry. Have the new ministry leader candidate attend the class too to answer specific questions pertaining to the new ministry.

    •   When pastors make the task of starting a new ministry a bit of trouble and perhaps difficult for the new leader, it's a form of test. How does this potential new leader cope with setbacks, regulations, having to comply with bylaws, and perhaps integrate with other ministers?

    •   As a pastor, you are intimately aware of the stresses involved in ministry, and you should be qualified to judge if the potential ministry leaders are ready for the job. Can they get along with this added responsibility and stress?

    •   If you are secure and confident that they are qualified and ready, go with it and support their efforts.

- If they are not, you have to be strong and let them know you do not feel they are ready. Offer to mentor them by giving them a less responsible position and see how they perform there. Then progressively move them up into leadership.

- Pastors are always in need of leaders and workers. Avoid the pitfalls of just appointing people simply because they have the desire but no proven ability to follow through to completion. Many people want to be the boss, but not everyone is qualified to be one.

3. Steps in creating the outline.

    - Draft a one-page, typewritten description of what the ministry will accomplish.

    - State the importance to the local body and the benefits it will receive by having this ministry in operation. Give examples of specific purpose that are short and to the point—no detail. For example, having Bible studies during the week, having a clean facility, or having trained ushers at every function.

    - Have them write the plan in an outline format similar to this manual. It will help them organize their thoughts and hopefully get them thinking of details they missed when they first got their idea.

    - An important point to cover is what the financial cost to the church will be. It might have to be a part of the church budget, so it requires serious thought. The leader should have an idea of where funds should come from or how they can be raised. It's easy to spend other people's money; those other people (the church membership) might like to see what you are spending it on. Depending on your church bylaws and rules, the church members might have to vote on the expenditure, so make the leaders have their facts and figures clearly stated in the outline.

4. The pastor should go over the first draft with the new leader and help him or her get it in a format where it can come to the church board for a vote (again if that is your procedure). At some point after the approval process, it should be posted on the bulletin board and introduced to the congregation at the next service. The pastor or the new leader should briefly introduce the new ministry and invite volunteers to join.

5. The final version should be incorporated into the local church's copy of this manual. Some churches might like to take this manual apart, three-hole punch it, and place it in a binder. Then it will be convenient for new leaders to take a copy of "their" chapters and tailor them to their needs. Add the final, approved versions of their chapters in the appropriate part of the manual at your church. Keep this original, so if rewrites are needed, the original and the modified versions are both available.

Contents and Format for the Outline

1. a one-page description of the ministry
2. dress and hygiene code
3. where and when the ministry will operate
4. description of individual tasks in detail, for example,

   - Members will clean and disinfect bathrooms after every service

   - Members will maintain the church premises mechanically and with the building trades to keep it in excellent condition. Members will contract out tasks that are impractical for volunteers to perform.

   - Members will provide flowers for every service and for people in the hospital. Members will organize and grow a Bible study group by inviting both members and other community members to attend. The goal is to split into new groups as each grows becoming an evangelistic outreach of the church.

5. Under each task, the detailed information has to be indicated.

   - For example, the location of cleaning equipment, which product to use where, who is to obtain replacement supplies, and how do they pay for them.

   - Lots of detail here because potential members have to have detailed instructions so they know what is expected of them and what the definition of a good job is!

   - All this detail is routine in the business world in which employees cannot be held to higher standards than those outlined in their job descriptions.

   - Likewise, as a church, we have to be specific about what we expect of our workers and expect godly diligence in the performance of their duties.

6. Who the leader and the chain of command are. It is disastrous to the ministry if people feel free to go to the pastor whenever they disagree with their ministry leader. See the chapter on church government for a detailed discussion.

CHAPTER 24

Suggested Church Financial Accountability Rules

We are supported by the tithes of our congregations. (Insert your bylaw reference for authority to make these rules.) Most churches have a requirement of members to be faithful in giving to the church. We take seriously the trust they have placed in us and covenant with them and with God to be good stewards of the resources entrusted to us.

Proper audit controls will be put in place so there is no appearance of evil or misunderstanding in the use of God's blessings. See 1 Thessalonians 5:22: "Abstain from all appearance of evil." We therefore adhere to the following rules of conduct in handling tithes and offerings.

1. Tithes and offerings shall be taken with a minimum of two ushers. In small groups, only one will collect while the other will stand by and assist in the count.

2. For Sunday services, two ushers will do the count under the supervision of the church secretary or member of the church board. Ushers will be rotated each Sunday so the same people do not count every offering.

3. For Sunday school, an older youth will be chosen each week to be the second counter and sign the Offering Counting Form. A different youth will be chosen each Sunday (or an usher can help). The Sunday school secretary treasurer will sign the third signature and turn over the offering to the church secretary.

4. All financial records and disbursements will be accounted for using the best accounting and bookkeeping programs available to the church secretary as advised by the accountant, CPA, or bookkeeping service employed by the church.

5. Records of giving shall be given to all contributors by either delivery at the church or mailing to the last known address of the contributor in January of each year.

6. We will be careful to adhere to state and federal guidelines for the accounting of gifts to preserve the tax deductions of the congregation and protect the tax-exempt status of the church.

7. We will deposit tax and payroll withholding monies due in the future in a separate account and hold it as a sacred trust to be rendered unto Caesar on time every time.

8. The fundraising policy of this church is that it is self-supporting and derives its income from free-will offerings of the congregation.

9. We will faithfully communicate the needs of the church to the congregation and believe that the Holy Spirit will move to urge us to contribute to the best of the abilities God has given us.

10. We believe in faith that as a Holy Spirit–led church, all our needs will always be met. Philippians 4:19: "And my God shall supply all your need according to His riches in glory by Christ Jesus."

11. Tithing is expected of all members. Tithe means "a tenth." God's plan to prosper us includes our faithful obedience to return a tenth to Him. We reject the notion that somehow the Old Testament blessing of the tithe somehow went away with the writing of the New Testament. Leviticus 27:30: "And all the tithe of the land, whether of the seed of the land or of the fruit of the tree, is the Lord's." It is holy to the Lord. We give our tithes to the Lord because they are His anyway. Jesus told us in Luke 6:38, "Give, and it will be given to you: good measure, pressed down, shaken together, and running over will be put into your bosom. For with the same measure that you use, it will be measured back to you." The tithe is a blessing from God and a way to give back to Him for all He has blessed us with; it is not just some burdensome religious duty.

12. Accordingly, a tenth of all the income of this local church shall be given as a tithe to other ministries, to missionaries, or to our denomination. All our local ministry needs shall be funded out of the 90 percent remaining.

Planning

13. A budget is essential to the proper stewardship of our church, and we will develop one every year and track our progress to make sure we stay on budget to the best of our ability. We will use prudent planning to forecast income and expenses.

14. We will graph the weekly tithe income for the past year, divide by the average adult attendance, and use those projections for formulating a new year's budget. We will adhere to our spending guidelines.

15. We will scrupulously and faithfully pay our bills on time every time.

Accounting

16. We will account for expenditures when purchasing any new equipment by using a purchase order and other expenses must be accounted for using expense vouchers. See also number 7 above. These rules follow.

17. Expense vouchers should be used when paying guest ministers and for reimbursing the pastor or other church members for expenses incurred on church business. (A copy of the suggested form is at end of this chapter.) They will also be used to reimburse payment for inexpensive items that are under the amount required for a formal purchase order.

18. In all cases, the receipt from the store or other vendor will be attached to verify the amount and keep the accounting accurate.

19. Purchase orders should be used for any purchase over an amount set by church policy. The pastor and any member purchasing anything over this amount must get a purchase order. (You can get these at any stationary store and stamp the church name on them. A large church will probably have them printed with church identification so it looks more professional.)

20. Avoid church charge accounts. If they must be used, limit the number of people who can use them, have strict accountability of every purchase, and have purchase orders for every item over the amount your finance committee decides.

Attached to this chapter are suggested formats for a designated funds policy and a sample Offering Counting Form.

Proposed Format for Policy for Receiving and Spending of Designated Funds

1. The (your church name) adopts this policy to comply with legal standards of charitable contributions. (Organize/number the form to comply with the format of your bylaws using proper paragraph and line numberings or heading. This should become a legal document.)

2. Some examples of legal compliance are:

   • "The contribution is unconditional and without personal benefit to the donor."
   • "The contribution is made 'to or for the use of' the church."
   • "The value of personal services is never deductible as a charitable gift."
   • "No deduction ordinarily is allowed unless the church exercises full administrative control over the donated funds to ensure that they are being spent in furtherance of the church's exempt purposes."

3. This should be a formal, recognized, and legal policy of the church. It is suggested that this document be made a part of your churches bylaws and be voted upon and understood by all members.

4. Givers are strongly encouraged to support first the unified budget of this local church with their regular tithes and other freewill offerings, not designating them for specific purposes. Designated gifts should be over and above the tithe.

5. This church will receive designated giving only for areas that are church approved or are already part of the church-approved unified budget. No designated gifts will be received until the church approves the proposed new fund. Tithe envelopes have the list of existing designated accounts on them for your convenience.

6. Each designated account must be approved in writing by the pastor and the advisory committee. All expenditures from any designated fund must have committee and pastoral approval ahead of time. Each expenditure will require a written report on how the money was used. These reports organized by specific account will become part of the regular annual finance report to the church.

7. Each designated account must be general in nature, for example: mission trips, missions offerings, evangelism, building improvement, new equipment, benevolence, scholarships, ministry projects, etc. and not specific in nature (a microphone fund, a rocking horse fund, a curtain fund, a hot tub fund, etc.)

8. Members' suggestions for the use of any donated funds may be considered, but the final decision must be based on the funds' best use in the context of the church's ministries. Members need to submit a written request to create a new designated-fund account.

9. When a designated gift does not fit into an account already established by the church, the donor will be contacted and asked if the gift can be used for a regular designated project. If the answer is no, the church must do one of three things.

   - create a new designated fund with appropriate accounting
   - advise the person to purchase the item and give it to the church with no strings attached or give the money with no strings attached
   - graciously decline the gift

10. Noncash gifts to the church will be acknowledged with a receipt that the donor can give to his tax professional. All noncash gifts become property of the church and may be used or sold at the church's discretion.

Offering Counting Form
(your church name)

Date _____

Event or Service (AM, PM, midweek, etc.) _____

Pennies	_____	@ $0.01	_____
Nickels	_____	@ $0.05	_____
Dimes	_____	@ $0.10	_____
Quarters	_____	@ $0.25	_____
1/2 dollars	_____	@ $0.50	_____
1 dollars	_____	@ $1.00	_____
	Total coins		$ _____

Ones	_____ $1	_____
Twos	_____ $2	_____
Fives	_____ $5	_____
Tens	_____ $10	_____
Twenties	_____ $20	_____
Fifties	_____ $50	_____
Hundreds	_____ $100	_____

Total currency $ _____

Total number of checks _____ Total amount of those checks $ _____

Total Offering $ _____

Counter _____

Counter _____

Counter _____

Three copies: one with deposit, one to pastor, one to church secretary treasurer

APPENDIX I TO THE MINISTRIES OF HELPS MANUAL

Copy of Adventures in Service to God
The Presenter's Manual

Adventures in Service to God
The Presenter's Manual for the Ministry of Helps
A Teaching Resource for Pentecostal and Charismatic Churches
Rev. Lawrence C. Spencer

A house is built by wisdom, and is set up by understanding. By discretion the chambers are filled with all precious and excellent wealth.

—Proverbs 24:3–4
(translated from the Septuagint, the Greek translation of the
Jewish Bible in use during the time of Jesus's ministry)

CONTENTS

FOREWORD

This manual is offered as a teaching resource to pastors who have the unique and nontransferable duties to "select (from among your church) seven (or more) reputable men filled with the Spirit and Wisdom to appoint to the task (of waiting tables ... workers)."

I stress that work in a church is not a substitute for faith, a prayer life, or for closeness to God. Working hard for God should be the *result* of these commitments to Him (see Acts 6:3).

This program gives you twelve weeks to look them over and listen to them. How do they act under pressure? Can they role-play a salvation prayer? If they can't, they'll never be able to do it in real life.

This training cannot teach them everything you as pastor would like them to know. However, this training gives you an opportunity to evaluate the spiritual maturity of the potential (or presently appointed) worker.

No other person is given this divine responsibility. The apostles did it themselves, and so pastors must do this training to assure themselves that every worker in their churches is spiritually mature and able to perform the rudimentary duties of pastoring or leading those working with them in their Helps jobs.

This Presenter's Manual contains all the text in the Participant's Manual and additional data to enable you to effectively teach the classes. Each participant must have a copy of the Participant's Manual; it's available where books are sold, including online.

As pastor, you should be intimately familiar with the topics. Read the entire manual before presenting it. Highlight what you want to read and paraphrase the rest. It is unlikely that you will find anything new or earthshaking in this manual. It is intended to provide you an organized way of presenting the material to stimulate discussion so you can evaluate individuals.

Words in **bold italics** are in places where there are blank spots in their manuals that they must fill in. So go slow at these points to give them a chance to write. Each lesson has hints and verbatim text if you choose to use it.

Important note: while the text of this manual is good teaching, your objective is to get to know the people whom you will potentially appoint to work in your ministry.

> Then the twelve summoned the multitude of the disciples and said, "It is not desirable that we should leave the word of God and serve tables. Therefore, brethren, seek out from among you seven men of *good* reputation, full of the Holy Spirit and wisdom, whom we may appoint over this business; but we will give ourselves continually to prayer and to the ministry of the word. (Acts 6:2–4)

As pastor and leader of your church, you are in effect summoning members of your church and selecting from among them those who meet the biblical standard. Get them engaged in discussion to find out who can fearlessly witness Jesus Christ and who will not participate. You may discover some folks who have issues in their lives that must be worked out before they get any formal responsibility in the church.

LESSON 1

Overview of the Helps Ministry

If you're not excited about what God is about to do in your life, you should be! For those who have been to Helps Training before, enjoy the review and join in the discussions. For those who are new, welcome to the world of foot washers and table servers. (Note: your assistants, associates, and appointed elders must attend the first class to set the example for the congregation.)

These classes will help fulfill the obligation God gives pastors and others in the fivefold ministry in Ephesians 4:11–14 to equip the saints, you, for saving souls. It will give you the foundation needed to minister to the needs of people in this local church and be better witnesses of Jesus Christ to a lost and dying world.

Materials Needed

- your Bible
- copies of the Code of Conduct (We will pass these out.)
- Participant's Workbook
- Helps Worker application (We will pass these out.)

The big gaps between entries in your manuals are reserved for you to fill in answers. When you go home, it is your responsibility to study the lesson we just presented and prepare for the discussion of the next lesson. We have put the scriptures in large type to make them easier to find.

The objectives of this first lesson are to show you a ministry ordained by God to unburden overworked pastors and to light the way for you to get involved in the body of Christ in a new and satisfying way. That is the Ministry of Helps. It has been with us since there was a church; it just didn't have the formal "Helps" name. A close name is "administrations" as cited in 1 Corinthians 12:28: "And God has appointed these in the church: first apostles, second prophets, third teachers, after that miracles, then gifts of healings, helps, administrations, varieties of tongues."

This first class will be the only one that is entirely lecture. This is to set the expectation both for you as participants and for ourselves as your leaders. We take responsibility for presenting the material, and it is your responsibility to read ahead and know the material each week.

Starting next week, we will have discussion groups at the beginning of the class so each of you has a chance to express yourself on all the topics. A pastor or other leader will join in each discussion group. That enables us as pastors and leaders to do our biblical responsibility of choosing from the flock those who are faithful and full of the Holy Spirit and wisdom to appoint over the various jobs in the church. It is essential that you read ahead and know what we will discuss and have something to add during the discussion.

We promise to do our job to the best of our abilities, and we expect you to participate and learn and understand your duties and responsibilities as Helps workers in this church.

Let's look at the Great Commission given to us by Jesus.

> And He said to them, "Go into all the world and preach the gospel to every creature. He who believes and is baptized will be saved; but he who does not believe will be condemned. And these signs will follow those who believe: In My name they will cast out demons; they will speak with new tongues; they will take up serpents; and if they drink anything deadly, it will by no means hurt them; they will lay hands on the sick, and they will recover." (Mark 16:15–18)

We are to go out and preach the good news. This can be accomplished only if we all do our part.

Why do we need an organized Helps Ministry? Among the multitude of challenges that face me as your pastor and the leadership of this church, two come quickly to mind. One, pastors like me feel they don't have enough time to do what they feel is needed. Second, the leadership and I have a burden for souls and seek to grow the church by getting new people saved.

Acts 6 tells us that the ancient church had the same challenges. It was even bringing strife to the local body at that time. What did they do? And what was the result?

Now we go to the fill-in part of the program. I'll let you know what to fill in. In the following weeks, we expect you to do the filling in at home after reading the lesson and looking up the scriptures. Each week, I or another instructor will call on some of you to tell me what you filled in after reading your Bible and researching the answers.

It is imperative that you do the homework. We do not have time in twelve lessons to read and discuss everything. As I stated before, we'll do our part, but you have to do your part too.

The apostles chose people they knew to have *wisdom* and *that had the baptism in the Holy Spirit*; they *appointed* them to do *practical ministerial duties so the apostles could minister the Word of God.* That is what we are doing here in this church. We are picking you out and making sure you are Spirit filled and wise so we can appoint you to positions in this church.

God's way is so simple. Our grandiose plans frequently waste time and get nothing done. I vote for God's way!

Acts 6:7 shows us the result of operating the ministry God's way. Three big things happened:

- The "Word of God increased"; more preaching and teaching occurred.
- The church grew in numbers; "the disciples multiplied." Not only that, but God gave them a bonus.
- Many Jewish priests became obedient to the faith. In those days, Christianity was an offshoot of Judaism, not a separate body. So converting a rabbi was a big deal. Converting people including Jewish people is still a big deal today.

The point here is that Acts 6:1–7 gives us our instructions. It shows us how to free up your pastor's time and how to grow the church. So let's not reinvent the wheel. God has given us specific instructions in his Instruction Manual, the Bible, so let's take His exhortation to heart and do what He tells us should be done. We'll discuss the practical aspects of this later.

Ephesians 4:11 admonishes me as your pastor and others in leadership to "prepare the saints for the work of the ministry." You are the saints, and we will prepare you for ministry.

The purpose of the Helps Ministry is to further the preaching of the gospel and the winning of new souls by delegating certain of the pastor's duties to the saints so those in a ministerial office as outlined in Ephesians 4:11 can get on with their appointed tasks. Similarly, the person serving in a lay ministerial office is outlined in Romans 12:27–28.

> Now you are the body of Christ, and members individually. And God has appointed these in the church: first apostles, second prophets, third teachers, after that miracles, then gifts of healings, helps, administrations, varieties of tongues.

All these gifts are for the work of the ministry, the Great Commission, and running a local church so the work can occur.

This passage gives us scriptural proof that Helps is divinely ordained to serve the church. Paul clearly placed the table workers and the church staff in some important company with the passages in verses 27–28. In this passage and Ephesians 4:11 and 1 Corinthians 12:7–11 are two new words: *helps* and *administration*. The KJV says "helps and governments"; a modern language Bible might say "help each other, and work together."

This shows us that the gifts of helping and administering in the church are on a par with the ministry and Holy Spirit gifts. Indeed, having a smooth-running church makes it much easier to usher in the moving of the Spirit. Back to verse 12.

- *prophets, apostles, and teachers* with evangelists and pastors omitted.
- *miracles, gifts of healing*, and *speaking in tongues* with wisdom, knowledge, faith, prophesy, discerning of spirits, and interpretation of tongues not mentioned.

Now you can fill the spaces in your workbook.

Neither God nor Paul ever wasted words. There is a reason workers and leaders (governments) are mentioned in the same breath as the ministers in the church and the gifts of the Holy Spirit—to elevate the practical workers' importance to the same level as the full-time ministry and the gifts of the Holy Spirit. Jesus taught extensively on not thinking of yourself as better than another because of your position such as sitting at the special place at a table and so on.

Those of us who are workers in God's church must be humble and serve the congregation as we would serve God Himself. Thus, this passage clearly seeks to place all of us on the same level.

There are three important Greek words used for "worker" in the NT. Two apply to lay workers and the third to the ministry.

- a *diakonos*, deacon, is a server, a waiter on the flock, a table server. In Mark 10:43, Jesus said whoever wanted to be great among you must be your servant.

- a *huperetes* is an underrower or seaman, later to signify anyone working "under" another. In Acts 26:16, it is used of Paul as a servant of Christ.
- The third word in common use was *leitourgos*, a public servant or minister. Jesus mentioned in Hebrews 8:2 "Minister of the Sanctuary," and in Romans 15:16, it was "a minister of Christ Jesus." We get the word *liturgy* from this.

Diakonos and huperetes are the words used in 1 Corinthians 12:28, not the third one. The emphasis was on the saints of the church becoming involved and doing the work of the ministry, which was as important as the ministerial gifts and the Holy Spirit gifts. There is no other logical or theological reason for this passage except to exhort us to greater works in God's service.

So our duties are clear: we are to win converts to Christ by assisting our pastor in our area (our world) in ministering to the people.

In Romans 16:1–16, Paul gave credit to many members of the Helps Ministry who assisted him in his missionary work. A fun exercise is to read these passages and substitute the names of local church helpers; that makes the Bible very personal. But it's personal to begin with, and it's the same today as it was yesterday and will be forever. Jesus is the Word. Wow, this is fun, isn't it?

Let's recap the important points so far. (You can fill these in in your workbook.)

- Mark 16:15 is for whom? *All saved people.*
- Acts 6 cites *how to choose members of the Helps Ministry.*
- Ephesians 4:11 *outlines the duties of our pastors and others in the fivefold ministry.*
- 1 Corinthians 12 *outlines the gifts of the Spirit*; in verse 28, he places workers with the Holy Spirit gifts and the ministry gifts and admonishes us to "eagerly desire the greater gifts."

Where Do We Get the Workers?

Now we get to the practicalities of Acts 6 in the Word.

(Instructor, read Acts 6:1–7.)

> In those days when the number of disciples was increasing, the Grecian Jews among them complained against the Hebraic Jews because their widows were being overlooked in the daily distribution of food. So the 12 gathered all the disciples together and said, "It would not be right for us to neglect the ministry of the Word of God in order to wait on tables. Brothers, choose seven men from among you who are known to be full of the Spirit and wisdom. We will turn this responsibility over to them and will give our attention to prayer and the ministry of the word." This proposal pleased the whole group. They chose Stephen, a man full of faith and of the Holy Spirit: also Philip, Procorus, Nicanor, Timon, Parmenas, and Nicholas from Antioch, a convert to Judaism. They presented these men to the apostles, who prayed and laid their hand s on them. So the

word of God spread. The number of disciples in Jerusalem increased rapidly, and a large number of priests became obedient to the faith. (Acts 6:1–7)

It is safe to assume that the apostles knew most of the seventy intimately and many others as very close associates. Jesus's ministry lasted only three years, and many were with him for much of that time. So the apostles probably had a large number of people to choose from to get seven men full of the Spirit and wisdom to wait on the tables of the widows.

In our world, where people move around a lot, we have a harder time finding qualified workers. It is a greater challenge for pastors to know potential leaders as intimately as Jesus and the apostles knew them in those days. So as leaders, we must use wisdom and seek out and train workers. This gives the opportunity to get to know you and to make the judgments needed to select the future leaders of the church. Perhaps future pastors!

This ministry training is the biblical method we chose to find people full of the Spirit and wisdom to put in Helps jobs in the local church. Here are the attributes we are looking for in workers

- born again and say so
- baptized in the Holy Spirit and have the evidence of speaking in tongues (Note: we can accomplish this now in the training program.)
- a trainable spirit, not argumentative (wise)
- obedient, a tither (wise)
- faithful in attendance
- willing to make a time commitment of twelve weeks of training and six months of service
- demonstrate Christian lifestyles (1 Timothy 3)
- sign and live up to the code of conduct while in the Helps Ministry

We have been careful to not make the list too long. We are looking for people with the right attitude, not perfection. This list was made up by us in this local church, so it is not infallible. We want you to fill these in the spaces in your workbook.

Some more fill-ins: Where the Bible is concerned, a rule is *absolute*; local custom is *flexible* as we in the leadership need it to be.

Recruits include anyone aspiring to full-time ministry. The Helps Ministry is wonderful training for workers in church organizations; they have less responsibility than they would have as full-time ministers. It's a great training ground for future pastors.

Anyone in Bible school should spend significant time in a Helps capacity. This will demonstrate faithfulness to a local body and allow the "fruits of their ministry" to be judged by the pastor and others supervising their education.

For regular members of the congregation, it offers a sense of belonging. For adults, it is a way of mentoring the younger generation. For the youth, it is a great way to take on responsibility in a structured way and learn skills needed in adulthood.

Training

This training course is the beginning. This is the first of twelve classes intended by me as your pastor to train you as present or future leaders in this local body. It is my responsibility and that of your leadership to know you have a certain level of biblical knowledge and some spiritual maturity as you minister to the flock God has assigned to us in this local church.

We are fulfilling our duty by creating this program to standardize the training locally so it complies with the Word of God and our vision for the church. In the small-group discussions, you can express yourself as a Christian and find the right spot for you to be the best Christian you can be. This will help pastors and leaders of this congregation to fulfill their biblical obligation to place faithful, wise, spirit-filled people in positions of responsibility in the church.

Those of you who are presently in ministry or are selected for ministry will also learn how to organize and supervise a function and train your replacements or stand-ins.

Many of you have a lot experience in ministry, but few of you have had formal training in how to run one. None of us knows how any local pastor wants to operate until that pastor first instructs them. This program will be taught by me as pastor and those on my leadership team.

As you complete the training, some of you as assistant and associate pastors will become trainers too. This is how Jesus ran His ministry, instructed the disciples and the seventy and others, and told them that they would do things in His name greater than even He had done. The church is sponsoring this program to instruct you in the skills needed to win souls and then send you out to do that.

Whether you are a musician, usher, nursery worker, or yard maintainer, you have the Great Commission, and your pastor has the responsibility to get you doing the work of the ministry. May God bless your studies, and may you faithfully complete them and obtain your certificate of completion.

One task that you will learn late in the instruction is how to plan and organize a ministry. Use this manual and remember the admonishment in the New Living Translation, *Proverbs 24:3–4: "A house is built by wisdom and becomes strong through good sense. Through knowledge its rooms are filled with all sorts of precious riches and valuables."*

Please copy this into your manual. It will help you remember an important Bible truth than can help you in ministry and in life in general. The three key words and phrases in this passage are *wisdom*, *common sense*, and *keeping abreast of the facts* (knowledge). Note that the context of this passage is not speaking of spiritual things per se; it is rather a practical admonition. It applies to our Helps jobs, our marriages, and our businesses or occupations. All three of these you can aspire to. You can seek, develop, and grow in all these areas.

This training program has been developed over thirty years of trial and error in many churches. We have prayed for wisdom. We've applied common sense where there was no biblical guidance. Our facts have been found in the Word, others, and our experiences. Let's dive in and get as much out of the classes as we can. We will all be the better for it. The Helps Ministry is a win-win proposition for everyone. It's biblical, it's practical, and it's fun.

Next week, we will discuss the Code of Conduct. Read it in your workbook and remember that it is for workers only; you do not have to adhere to any Code of Conduct to attend this church.

This is not a secret document, but it is not for general sharing with church members because someone may make the mistake of thinking it is required of members. Only workers who voluntarily sign the Code of Conduct must follow it. Write your questions in your workbook and be ready to discuss the code next week.

In each lesson, the scriptures are printed in large type. Your homework is to look them up and read them and perhaps bookmark them. As we discuss them, you will find them easily.

We have finished our first week. God bless you all. We'll see you all Sunday for church and next week for the class, same time same station.

(Instructor: pick someone for a closing prayer. Items in italics are instructions for you, not text to read to the class. In future lessons, some sentences will be delineated by bullets ; these are talking points. If they are not discussed in the small groups, you can bring them up as you see fit after the discussions.

Remember, you can read the lessons verbatim if you wish. But the real reason is stimulating discussion to see if the attendees have read their lessons—wisdom—and if they can apply the teaching full of the Holy Spirit, the Enabler.

The Helps Training program is more effective and has more credence if you can get all pastors and senior leadership to attend the first class. Leaders lead by setting the example. Where I have conducted the class, the pastor always attended every meeting of the first session; thereafter, he or she or an associate conducted some of the classes. Pastors have to stay involved to get to know the workers personally.)

LESSON 2

Setting the Example

Instructor Information

This class will begin with a discussion of the Code of Conduct. Note who in the class participates and who does not. Who read the lesson and who did not? Who made notes and has questions and who did not? Those who take the training seriously will handle their volunteer jobs diligently. The converse is also true.

This training program is an opportunity for the pastor and leadership to carefully and wisely pick people who are wise enough to participate and full of the Holy Spirit to appoint over these important volunteer Helps positions.

After the discussion, you can go over some talking points just to emphasize the code and why we use it.

Break them up into groups of six or seven. Place an elder or assistant or associate pastor as group leader. If the class is small, you can keep them all together. If you have multiple groups, have one member present two minutes of highlights. Have a different member do the discussion each week.

(Instruction starts here.)

You will stay in the same group for the entire twelve weeks. Another leader or I will lead each group. We will switch which group we sit in every week so we can get an opportunity to get to know every participant and end up feeling good about judging your wisdom, faithfulness, and infilling of the Holy Spirit. Discussions will stop after twenty minutes or so.

During this training and while you work in Helps, you will be judged. Acts 6:3 requires us to judge you, to pick you for workers in the ministry, so we will do so. The Bible also admonishes the saints (you and all the others in the church) to respect (know) those who work hard among you. So both you and your leadership will be judged (known) by the congregation (1 Thessalonians 5:12).

As leaders, we will be looked at critically by the congregation and visitors to see if we measure up to their idea of what a Christian leader should be. So we have developed a Code of Conduct that we voluntarily live by to help us stay on the straight and narrow path. Remember (stress this!), the Code of Conduct is for workers, leaders, and paid staff only.

At the close of this class, we will pass out a one-page code we have adopted for our use. You can sign it now or take it home and discuss it with your spouse. If your family is not in agreement, don't sign it. As a local church, we can require compliance with a formal written code of only committed workers, paid staff, and Bible students. Only those who have signed the Code of Conduct can be required to live by it.

Judgment stops with the paid staff, ministerial candidates, leadership, and volunteer workers. We must love all the people attending the church; we will evaluate their spiritual walks and disciple them to the degree they will allow it, but we do not judge them by dress, looks, or lifestyles. If the sinner cannot find a home with us, where they can be loved into repentance, where would they find it? At a bar?

Our example is Jesus. He supped with publicans and sinners. He was criticized by the church folk for not hanging out with a better class of people. Sometimes in Christian churches, people who do not smell good, have tattoos and body piercings, wear weird clothes, and so on are not made to feel welcome. What would He have done if Matthew would have had a tattoo and worn his baseball cap backward? Would Jesus not have chosen him? I think not. We have to judge the inner person when we evaluate someone for service in the Helps Ministry. We hope that as we live up to the code, our conduct as workers and leaders will be an example to the congregation of a better lifestyle in Christ.

Please understand that this code is not for distribution to the members of the congregation. It's no big secret, but they might get the wrong idea that they have to comply with it to be members or attendees of the church. This is not the case as you know. We welcome all in our church regardless of their current lifestyles. Our charge is to reconcile them with Jesus Christ and love them into fellowship with God with the Word of God, not beat them on the head with a heavy family Bible or judge them by the Code of Conduct we apply only to ourselves.

Code of Conduct

I hope everyone has read the scriptures for this week. As you will see, everything on the list is inspired by biblical principles. Some are directed at deacons or other leaders. We have incorporated them into this Code of Conduct so all our workers can aspire to a better Christian walk.

Look at the Code of Conduct, and let's learn the biblical basis that inspired them in 1 Timothy 3. There are also other biblical references. Paul's letter to Timothy gives us an outline that we have rounded out with other exhortations from the Word.

Speak in One Accord with the Leadership (1 Corinthians 1:10)

The congregation must see all of us supporting the pastor and enthusiastically pursuing his vision for the local congregation. Any differences of opinion are to be discussed in Helps Ministry training classes like this one or privately with the person involved (Matthew 18:15–17).

For purposes of the Helps Ministry, we expect you to first contact your group leader if you have a problem even if it is with him or her. If you don't get satisfaction, go to that person with another member of the team who agrees with you as a witness. If you still aren't satisfied, go to that person's supervisor. If you are not still not satisfied, drop the matter. It's not okay to go to the pastor. You must give your leaders latitude to do things differently than you might prefer and be ready to forgive them for their mistakes.

Live a Clean Life (1 Corinthians 6:19–20)

I will not defile the temple of God (my body) with smoking, drinking alcoholic beverages, using illicit drugs, or engaging in immoral sex or other unhealthy practices. This should be a no-brainer, but many think that it's okay to indulge in these things as long as they "love" Jesus. You may be a work in progress, and some in the church may drink and smoke, etc., but if you are going to be in Helps, you cannot.

Clean of Body and Breath (1 Timothy 3:2)

As an example of self-control and respectability, I will keep myself clean of body and breath and dress in clean and appropriate clothing as a living example of how Jesus would have me look as His representative on earth.

We are His only witnesses. How we look, smell, and conduct ourselves is how He is judged by the unsaved and the baby Christians. This item is all about example.

On Time (Matthew 24:45–46)

I will faithfully be on time and attend all church services when I am scheduled to work. I will never miss a function I am scheduled to work at without getting a substitute. (emergencies excepted).

It would be nice if all workers made every activity, but that is not reasonable. However, remember our priorities; we cannot ignore time with God, family, or your employment just to have a perfect attendance record at church.

Reliable (Proverbs 18:9)

1. I will be reliable and dependable on my assigned job. When I sign up, I will be there to work. It is much better to not sign up rather than let the pastor believe a job will be done then not show up (Proverbs 12:17). Ouch. Remember, in this church, we make six-month commitments; after that, you can reenlist. If your job is not for you, you can try another or rest in the congregation and reenlist when time permits.

2. I agree to tell my supervisor if I am being used too much, not wait until I burn out and quit in anger (Matthew 18:15).

3. I will complete all training even if I have heard it before (Proverbs 13:16, 15:5, 15:32, 19:20). (Please keep an open mind and a trainable attitude. I do not know of anyone who has memorized all the scriptures mentioned in this training program. There are

instructors who have taught this program many times and learn something new every time.)

4. I agree to make myself available as an exhorter if needed even if my job is behind the scenes and not with people. Jesus gave us all the Great Commission to preach the gospel, and I must be instant in season to be able to witness salvation, healing, baptism in the Holy Spirit, and deliverance. If the pastor or other leader calls, I agree to serve as an exhorter or usher or any other job at any time I am needed during a service (1 Timothy 4:13; 2 Timothy 4:2, and many others).

5. I agree to tithe 10 percent of my finances and of my time to God and diligently pray for my family, church, country, secular job, and all humanity (Hebrews 7:1–10; Malachi 3:8–11). (Under the new covenant, we can tithe more than 10 percent. People who aspire to the Helps Ministry must be tithers. We would like all to tithe into this body to further the work locally; however, we will not be checking. When you put in your application, the church secretary will check to make sure you are a regular giver.)

6. I agree to obey the leadership without question during any organized service. (The Holy Spirit places leaders in place. An organized service is an inappropriate place to question authority or anointing. Save your questions or suggestions for training sessions or at a time other than at an organized service; read Titus 3:1).

7. I agree to take the time to get "prayed up" so I can be operating supernaturally in the will of God on my Helps job. (This is also a good practice on your secular job. When worldly things happen that make you uncomfortable, the Holy Spirit can bring "all things to remembrance" to help you through the difficult time; John 14:26).

8. As a favor to my Pastor, I agree to accept temporary assignments in other jobs to fill needs until someone else is found. (This should seldom happen. Three weeks will be the limit of substitutions, not the normal six-month commitment.)

9. I agree to keep my children under control as an example to other parents and so mine don't lead others astray (1 Timothy 3:4).

10. I will faithfully live and study the Word of God to the best of my ability to show my self approved so I can be an example of prosperity and great success according to 2 Timothy 2:15 and Joshua 1:8.

At the end of the single-page code, there is a place for your signature. "I agree to abide by this Code of Conduct as a Helps worker or staff member of this church." Again, consider your decision carefully and prayerfully. No one needs to sign now. Your signature is your word that you will follow the code for the period of time you are serving in Helps. It also signifies that you voluntarily hold yourself accountable to the pastor and those who serve in leadership of the church.

(Instructor: you need ten minutes to close this lesson and introduce the next one.)

We have two quick things before we introduce the next lesson. First, some questions. Class, please answer aloud.

- The Code of Conduct is for paid staff and workers only. True or false?
- We judge people attending church by their dress. True or false?

(Instructor: a recap of lessons 1 and 2.)

The first two lessons laid the foundation for the course. In them, we learned about the Great Commission, the big reason churches exist—to bring converts to Jesus and then disciple them.

We were reminded how the fivefold ministry has the responsibility and obligation to prepare the saints to carry out the Great Commission. We discovered how Helps was ordained by God. We learned that we have to choose people for Helps. We are now experiencing the training method the local church has chosen to select, choose, train, and equip helpers. We discussed the way we set the example for the church members by voluntarily abiding by the Code of Conduct.

Finally, a preview of lessons 3 to 6. The next series of lessons emphasizes four foundational concepts that are generally accepted as being important for all workers to know well. Over the next four weeks, our objective is to have you become very comfortable witnessing these topics to the unsaved or to other Christians and doing so in a loving, caring manner.

Some churches have entitled this "counselor" training. We disagree with that terminology because it is not biblical. Do not use that term when speaking to others about Bible topics. The proper terminology is "exhorter training."

Next week, we will study exactly why we use the term *exhorter training* and start a very spiritual and enjoyable part of the training.

(Notes to instructor: before closing, remind the class that it is their responsibility to read next week's lesson and be prepared to discuss it during the first twenty minutes of class. Instructors or group leaders should take notes on items or people's comments that the pastor needs to know such as concerns or attitudes out of the ordinary. Go over each item briefly; they were supposed to study them on their own. If people do not study the homework or read ahead, that is an indication of their work habits in Helps Ministry. You need to discern if they are wise enough to realize they need to study, and if they are not diligent, either retrain them or let them go in love.)

What we are looking for is joyful compliance, so immediately identifying and delivering anyone of a rebellious or dissident spirit from the group is essential to having an effective group setting. We have experienced old hands absolutely refusing to do homework as they considered that below their station and position in the church. They have to be admonished that they are the example, and if they refuse, others may follow their lead.

We have also had to lovingly release people from longtime service because they were unable or unwilling to accept the new training and organization. You have to exercise tough love or your training program, indeed your entire Helps Ministry, will be in jeopardy.

If this is your first time introducing an organized Helps Ministry in your church, be prepared for these challenges. I guarantee there will be someone who feels too good to have to put up with going through training after so many years of service.

Good luck. You will need it!)

(close in prayer)

LESSON 3

Born Again——A Gift from God

Welcome to lesson 3. This is the first of four foundational lessons in the Helps Ministry Training Program. I hope you have studied the information in this lesson and are prepared to discuss the topic in this session. My goal is to get you comfortable in winning souls to Christ. As we go over today's material, I hope you will share with us your concerns and challenges you have had in witnessing salvation to someone.

A lively class discussion with everyone being candid in his or her remarks will help us all in the practical application of the information in the lesson. The Helps Ministry exists to win souls and provide a place where discipleship can occur. We cannot do the work God has assigned to each of us well unless we prepare.

Each lesson in this series is important and foundational to a vibrant Helps Ministry and a local church prepared to minister to those God entrusts to us.

(Instructor: begin twenty or so minutes of discussion After the discussion, here are some talking points.)

Remember, when we pray for someone, explain Bible concepts to them, or admonish them, we are acting as exhorters of the Word, not counselors. Everyone, say, "I am an exhorter!" Write it in the margin of your workbook. In this church, we do not use the word *counselor* except to describe the activities of a professionally licensed individual.

The only way anyone is ever born again is through faith in Jesus Christ (Ephesians 2:8). That faith comes by hearing and understanding the Word of God (Romans 10:17), not by our eloquence, opinions, or experiences.

Most of this chapter is a transcription of an actual (fairly long) Bible tract. There are many good tracts in circulation, and many are available at Christian bookstores. I suggest you find one you like, learn it thoroughly, and have it handy.

The words *born again* have been misunderstood by many people for many years. Religious people sometimes feel it applies only to those who don't have a good academic understanding of what church is all about. They may confine the term to what Baptists or Pentecostals believe. Others consider it a term made popular by evangelists on radio or TV. These and all other nonbiblical explanations are wrong.

Born again is not a term invented by any religion or denomination. Jesus himself coined the phrase in John 3:1–21.

(Instructors, during the group discussions, if someone does not bring up the following, you should do it. You will run into traditional explanations such as, "I was baptized a _____, so I will go to heaven." "I was baptized when I was a baby, so I will go to heaven." "I work diligently in my church and obey all the church doctrine, so I will go to Heaven." Wrong. A lot of honest, hard-working, loyal, good-parenting, nondrug-using, and patriotic people are going straight to hell when they die. Hosea 4:6 says it all: "My people are destroyed for lack of knowledge.")

We pray to God that as you complete this training, you will get a passion for souls and not want anyone you know to go to hell for lack of the knowledge of the way to heaven—salvation.

(Instructor: start the tract.)

In the Bible, a Jewish religious leader highly respected in the community commented on the miracles Jesus was performing. Jesus did not acknowledge his words; instead, He replied, "Unless you are born again you cannot see the Kingdom of God." Nicodemus was that religious man. He then started discussing being born again with Jesus. Perhaps he was trying to understand what being born again meant.

Today, many people are still missing the point of Jesus's works—that you must believe by faith, not your mind—the blessing God has provided us.

Jesus told Nicodemus that we are born once from our mothers' wombs, born of water. Being born again is a personal, spiritual choice we make to believe in Jesus Christ as our Lord and Savior. Jesus explained this in John 3:16 and 3:36, and Paul elaborated on the choice in Romans 10:9–17. Read these and make them a part of yourself. In 2 Corinthians 5:17, we learn that if anyone is in Christ, he or she becomes new creatures. This means that the old us—the sinners, the failures, the dissatisfied parts of us—is passed away. In Jesus, we become new spirits.

We are spirits; we have minds (emotions/intellects), and we live in bodies, which don't usually change. We have to take control of our flesh with our souls and spirits.

Jesus was brutally beaten and crucified; He shed His blood for our sins. He went to hell and defeated Satan for us! He was raised form the dead by God, preached for a while, and went to heaven to be with God. He sits at the right hand of the Father preparing a place for you in heaven. He is reaching out to you now through these words and through the person who gave you this tract.

You receive the new birth by faith through the grace of God. You cannot earn it through religious service, teaching Sunday school, doing good works, being honest, or even through the intercession of a member of the clergy. Read Ephesians 2:8–10 and see that good works are the result of being born again, not a requirement for it.

You will find that being born again is a gift from God. John 3:16 tells us, "God so loved the world (including you and I) that He gave his only Son (Jesus) so that anyone (not just the good people, but everyone) who believes in Him will not perish but will have eternal life (with Jesus in Heaven)." Wow!

You can have it too! You can receive Jesus Christ as your personal Savior right now. You can have eternal life for yourself in heaven. You can also begin to learn His promises for the abundant and healthy life He has for you on earth now. Pray the prayer of salvation right now aloud; don't delay another minute. Say this prayer to God, believe it in your heart, and speak it with your lips.

Dear God, I believe that Jesus Christ is Lord, that he was born as a man, was crucified for me, died, went to hell, and defeated the Devil for me. Then God, you raised him from the dead, and He is sitting at Your right hand. I confess Jesus as my personal Lord and Savior. I confess my sins and repent of them. I know you are faithful to forgive me of all my sins. I receive my forgiveness by faith and thank you that I am now born again, a new person in Jesus Christ. In His name I pray, amen.

Praise God! You did it. You just became a born-again believer. You are a new creature (new creation) in Jesus Christ not because you look or feel like one but because God says so. Now that you are a new Christian, you have all the rights and promises in the Bible. You also take on all the responsibilities of a Christian. You will always have the freedom of choice; you can do it God's way or your way. Romans 12:2 admonishes us to renew our minds.

A good start is reading the Bible to discover what God has to say about how to live your life. Remember, the Bible is the only infallible reference for how we are to live our lives. Reject the worship or hold in reverence or practice any tradition or teaching that does not line up with the Word of God.

Change what you put in your mind every day. Read things about your occupation, your health, and some Christ-centered literature (Christian bookstores have a lot of it). Changing what you feed your mind will help make you the better person you want to be. You will become a new person outwardly as well as spiritually. Strive to be better on the job as a worker or supervisor, better at home as a parent or as a daughter or son. You will be better equipped to pass on this great gift of salvation to others.

Be a better person, and when people wonder why, tell them what happened to you; tell them about Jesus, who saved you and can save them too! In 2 Timothy 2:15, the apostle Paul sent a strong message to Timothy: "Study to show himself approved." That same message is good for us today.

Next, share this tract with others so they have a chance to know Jesus too. In Mark 16:15, Jesus told us to go out into the world and preach the gospel to every creature. You may know only what is in this tract and what has happened to you, but you can witness (preach) what you know to others and help them build their faith and accept Jesus Christ as their personal Lord and Savior. You can do it, and God will bless your efforts.

Finally, join a church that openly and joyfully preaches the uncompromised Word of God. Many churches water down the Word; they say that miracles are not for today, or they may mix the Bible with some other sacred book or denominational teaching. Beware of those who claim that some people or group has revelation not in the Bible and that you have to obey their teachings.

In Galatians 1:8, Paul dealt with churches, denominations, people, and even angels who used teachings not in the Bible to set religious doctrine: "But even if we or an angel from heaven, preach any other gospel to you than what we have preached, let him be accursed (let him go to hell)." Wow!

Remember, what is preached and taught are important, not denominational labels. If you are told that some parts of the Bible are "not for today," run, don't walk, away.

Pray for God's Holy Spirit to reveal to you where you should worship. Your spiritual life depends on the food (the teachings) the man or woman of God feeds you. Choose carefully, take notes, and go home and check the notes with the Word of God. If that is the right place for you, then join, become a diligent worker, and tithe honestly and faithfully; God will bless your obedience to His Word.

(Instructor: this should be brought up in the discussion if one of the students doesn't.)

It is imperative that once you have had the honor of praying with someone for salvation, you follow up and see to it that he or she gets involved in a Jesus-believing church. This may be here at our church; perhaps another one. But let's not abandon new believers and risk backsliding because we failed to point them to a church for follow-up. Remember Mark 4:15: Satan comes immediately to steal the Word that was sown in their hearts.

Here are other great salvation scriptures you might want to jot down.

> But as many as received Him, to them He gave the right to become children of God, to those who believe in His name: 13 who were born, not of blood, nor of the will of the flesh, nor of the will of man, but of God. (John 1:12)

> For God so loved the world that He gave His only begotten Son, that whoever believes in Him should not perish but have everlasting life. (John 3:16)

> For all have sinned and fall short of the glory of God, being justified freely by His grace through the redemption that is in Christ Jesus, whom God set forth as a propitiation by His blood, through faith, to demonstrate His righteousness, because in His forbearance God had passed over the sins that were previously committed, to demonstrate at the present time His righteousness, that He might be just and the justifier of the one who has faith in Jesus. (Romans 3:23–26)

> But God demonstrates His own love toward us, in that while we were still sinners, Christ died for us. (Romans 5:8)

> For the wages of sin is death, but the gift of God is eternal life in Christ Jesus our Lord. (Romans 6:23)

> But God, who is rich in mercy, because of His great love with which He loved us, even when we were dead in trespasses, made us alive together with Christ (by grace you have been saved). (Ephesians 2:4–5)

> For by grace you have been saved through faith, and that not of yourselves; it is the gift of God, not of works, lest anyone should boast. (Ephesians 2:8–9)

> If we confess our sins, He is faithful and just to forgive us our sins and to cleanse us from all unrighteousness. (1 John 1:9)

(Instructor: these are your closing remarks. Questions? Comments?)

Next week, we will discuss baptism in the Holy Spirit. Please read your lesson ahead of time. Most of us have heard many sermons on this topic and have seen people be baptized in the Holy Spirit and may think we have seen and heard it all concerning this baptism. Read ahead anyway and keep an open mind for new ways of ministering to others.

The purpose of this next lesson is to get all of us comfortable with praying someone through the baptism, not just being watchers but doers of the Word. We will have practical application of praying for someone and having them be baptized in the Holy Spirit.

If any of you has a family member or know anyone inside or outside the congregation who is interested in being baptized in the Holy Spirit, invite him or her to the next class. Children are welcome. Tell them we give a written guarantee that they will get baptism in the Holy Spirit if they earnestly desire it and are open to the Holy Spirit. See the guarantee for yourself in 1 Corinthians 12:7 and Luke 11:13.

(closing prayer and dismissal)

LESSON 4

Baptism in the Holy Spirit

This lesson is the second in the training of workers to be exhorters of the Word of God. Many new people are eager to receive salvation; that's pretty standard in the Christian tradition. Believing in Jesus and confessing Him as our Savior is fairly universal over the Christian denominations. It's called by different names, but it is acceptable. Baptism in the Holy Spirit does not enjoy this widespread acceptance. Some denominations will expel you if they find out you are baptized in the Holy Spirit. Others ignore the parts of the Bible that teach on the charismatic gifts.

So witnessing to new converts about baptism in the Holy Spirit could be resisted because of false teaching they have or prejudices they may harbor. We must, therefore, be mindful of Paul's teaching in 1 Corinthians 1:1–3; we must approach the new convert or the person who resists the teaching with love.

The first recipients of baptism in the Holy Spirit were given the promise and told by Jesus after the resurrection to stay in Jerusalem and in a few days they would be baptized with the Holy Spirit. This instruction tells us that Jesus was giving His people a choice. If they chose not to stay, they could go on as they were, go to heaven, etc. But if they chose to stay, if they earnestly desired baptism in the Holy Spirit, they would be "clothed with power from on high" (Luke 24:49).

In John 16:5 and following, Jesus went into detail in promising the Holy Spirit, the Counselor, the Spirit of truth to give the disciples power to do the work of bringing people to Jesus. Check out verse 8: "When he (the Holy Spirit) comes, he will convict the world of guilt in regard to sin and righteousness and judgment."

In Luke 11:13, Jesus promised the Holy Spirit to anyone who asked. This is a key scripture; Jesus was making a promise to everyone today, and He did it over 2,000 years ago. Hebrews 13:8 says Jesus is the same yesterday, today, and forever. His testimony is truth and life. Therefore, when we witness to folks to aid them in receiving baptism in the Holy Spirit, it is important to remember these scriptures especially if we don't have a tract handy.

Remember that the Word works! We may have great opinions and interesting experiences to impart, but everything we have is weak compared to the power of the Living Word of God, your Bible.

So let's go to a tract. In a few minutes, we will get some people up front and have receivers and prayers. The receivers will get baptism in the Holy Spirit. I hope we have some people in the group who earnestly desire baptism, people who are obedient Christians and love Jesus, born-again Christians who desire the power Jesus promised more than anything. If so, they can receive it from Jesus here tonight.

If we don't have anyone needing baptism, we need some volunteers to be the receivers.

Instead of getting it for the first time, they can get another infilling of Jesus' power and become even more effective witnesses.

Before we start, we need to go over the first part of the tract. If you are praying with someone after a service, you need to find out where they are in the Word. How much of the altar-call preaching do they remember? The first few paragraphs of the tract are instructional and help them understand baptism. The paragraphs after the prayer give them more understanding as to what happened and what they can expect.

I'll read the first portion, then we will bring the folks up front, and they definitely will receive the Holy Spirit baptism!

When you come up, expect to receive; this is not pretend tonight. We don't play Bible. This is going to be one of the most memorable times of someone's life in a few minutes. Thank you, Jesus, for sending us the Holy Spirit.

A Copy of the Tract *Baptism in the Holy Spirit*—A Gift That IS for Today!

There are over 600 references to the Spirit in the Bible. He is the third person of the Trinity—Father God, Jesus God, and God the Holy Spirit. Many of these references refer to the Holy Spirit and the power He gives to people. This short study will start with John the Baptist's prophesy of a baptism in the Holy Spirit the Messiah will bring.

This is promised in all four gospels: Matthew 3:11, Mark 1:8, Luke 3:16, and John 1:33 and at least twenty other places in the New Testament. John's prophesy carries much authority since Jesus described him by saying, "There is not a greater prophet than John The Baptist" (Luke 7:26–28).

After His resurrection, Jesus again promised the Holy Spirit. At Pentecost, 120 people including Mary, Jesus' earthly mother, and his brothers received baptism in the Holy Spirit. Further, they all began to speak in unknown tongues! It must have sounded weird—a lot of adults babbling baby talk. The Bible tells us that many foreign visitors in Jerusalem heard this babbling as their own native tongues! Others who didn't speak these languages heard it and thought the 120 were drunk on wine. Of the people who heard it in their own language, many were saved. Acts 2 gives us the history of this first day. After the original 120 got baptism, others received it by faith quickly when prayed with by one of the Spirit-baptized people.

The people who judged the situation in worldly terms probably still thought they were drunk or a bunch of fanatics. In Acts 2:40–41, Peter pleaded with people to repent, suggesting that some did not heed his pleading. In verse 42, we read, "those who accepted …" indicating some did not accept Jesus; they were not saved or baptized in the Holy Spirit.

So make sure your candidates have accepted Jesus, are sold out, have repented of their sins, and want to live as a testimony to Jesus. No one is perfect, but make sure they are sincere. Remember verse 41—"those who accepted …" There is no faking baptism in the Holy Spirit. If you earnestly want it, Jesus promises it to you, and you will receive.

The setting of praying with someone could be after an altar call when a group prayer was offered for baptism, or in a personal setting, or anywhere you find a person desiring the gifts. We need to be ready to assist no matter what our church function is.

There are nine gifts of the Holy Spirit given by Jesus for us to do the work He set out for us to do. We received the right to receive the gifts when we accepted salvation. However, being immersed or baptized in the Holy Spirit is a separate act of grace. Jesus promised the gift to us. It is ours today if we earnestly seek the Holy Spirit and obediently follow Jesus.

Usually, we don't receive baptism when we receive salvation because the person who prayed with us for salvation told us only enough of the Word to get us to the place we could believe in Jesus and accept Him as our personal Savior. Not hearing the Word of God concerning baptism equals no knowledge that the gift exists, and usually, this equals not getting baptism. Some people are saved and baptized in the Holy Spirit by reading a tract like this one. Praise God, we hope you will too. But most often, it's a Christian who teaches you about the gifts and prays with you until you receive them.

Faith (for salvation, baptism in the Holy Spirit, or anything else) comes by hearing and understanding God's Word, the Bible (Romans 10:17). If there is no preaching about the Spirit, people won't learn about or receive baptism in the Holy Spirit. This tract is to make up for preaching you never heard or didn't understand. Take this information and believe with all your heart that Jesus will baptize you in the Holy Spirit, and He will. You need to be obedient, to hunger for, and to believe you will receive. You do your part, and He will do His part.

Speaking in tongues is the initial outward sign that you have received baptism in the Holy Spirit. So much of this tract is devoted to that topic. The other gifts are for your further Bible study or another class later on. On the day of Pentecost, some judged tongues harshly and criticized the Christians, and that still goes on today. There are sincere Christians who misinterpret the Bible and believe that tongues are not for today, or worse, are of the devil!

However, the Bible tells us that Jesus is the same yesterday, today, and forever (Hebrews 13:8). Jesus is still baptizing people in the Holy Spirit, and we are still speaking in tongues! Nothing has changed. Christians are still operating in the supernatural gifts of the Holy Spirit, and we are still being judged by religious people. Follow Jesus and believe what God says through the Bible, not what others say it says.

All the gifts of the Spirit revealed to us in 1 Corinthians 12–14 are for us today. We will continue to need and rely on these gifts until the revelation of God's will is perfect, when the gospel is complete. We look to Revelation 21; God's Bible tells us that the final perfection will be when God dwells with us and we with Him. Obviously, there will be no need for spiritual gifts then because He will be with us.

Until that time, Jesus' Great Commission in Mark 16:15–20 is still in operation. We must be obedient to Jesus' instructions to go out in the world and tell everyone about Him. The Holy Spirit is the enabler, through the spiritual gifts, for us to be more-effective witnesses of Jesus Christ. To obediently do the job He told us to do using the gift he promised us to enable us to be good witnesses. When Jesus returns, the gospel will be complete, not before.

Baptism in the Holy Spirit, like salvation, is a gift God promised us. He doesn't give any bad gifts; He loves us too much. We can receive baptism in the Holy Spirit right now! Jesus said in Luke 11:13 that God would give the Holy Spirit to those who ask Him, and that means anyone who earnestly seeks the gift and asks Jesus sincerely for the gifts. He will baptize him or her in the Holy Spirit.

So pray this prayer out loud to God. Believe in faith that He will baptize you in the Holy Spirit and that you will speak in an unknown tongue.

> Dear God: I come to you as a born-again believer in Jesus Christ. I believe you raised Him from the dead and He is in heaven with you now. I confess Him as my Lord and Savior. I ask for baptism in the Holy Spirit. I declare to you that I will receive it in faith and use my mouth to speak in a tongue I cannot understand.
>
> In Jesus' name, I cast out any spirit of fear, unbelief, prejudice, or embarrassment that would try to hinder me. I replace it with a spirit of faith in your promise to give me baptism in the Holy Spirit if I asked you for it. So right now, in Jesus' name, I receive by faith baptism in the Holy Spirit.

Now that you have been baptized in the Holy Spirit, whether you are alone or praying with someone, close your eyes, praise God, and thank Him for baptizing you in the Holy Spirit. God inhabits the praise of his children. Continue praising Him. Praise Him and thank Him in a language you have never spoken. Control your tongue and speak words of faith in a language you don't know. Do it in faith. You have to move your tongue and lips; you have to talk. Say something in faith.

What you are doing here is described in 1 Corinthians 14:15, praying to God in your own understanding (your native language) and praying to Him in the Spirit (or a language you don't know, also called your prayer language). What you are doing is entirely biblical, so praise Him in faith.

Later on in your private prayer time, praise Him often in tongues daily for five minutes or so. Make it a sacrifice of praise to God for blessing you with salvation and baptism in the Holy Spirit.

There are four types of tongues revealed to us in the Word of God. (On the actual tract they will be printed in the text; here, they are blank so you can fill them in to help you remember them.)

1. A way to speak with God, or _____ _____. See 1 Corinthians 14:2, 4, 14 and Jude 20.

2. Tongues _____, for exhortation, as a sign for the unbeliever. See 1 Corinthians 14:22, 26, 27, 28.

3. Tongues as a _____. This happened at Pentecost when the visitors to Jerusalem heard the newly Spirit-baptized believers speaking in the listener's native language. See Acts 2:4, 5, 6.

4. And _____. A manner of praying in situations in which we are so overcome that we cannot think of the appropriate words. The Spirit gives utterance here, and we do not have control of what comes out of our mouths. See Romans 8:26.

God has provided tongues as a gift. He expects you to use it for His glory. Some denominations and some people do not believe in tongues or any of the other gifts of the Holy Spirit mentioned in 1 Corinthians 12:8, 9, 10. Keep in mind that people's opinions, preferences, or prejudices do not nullify or modify the Word of God, which is fact; people's interpretations of it are frequently incorrect.

Some people fear that tongues or other gifts of the Spirit may be misused as they were in Corinth in Paul's time, so they don't teach about them. Others out of incorrect teaching, ignorance, tradition, or some other reason feel that the gifts aren't real or aren't for today. Please read the Bible; believe what God says to you through the written Word. Believe what Jesus said He would do. Reject teaching to the contrary. Do not fear or reject the gifts God wants to give you. Praise Him for all the gifts, and give each the reverence and respect a God-given gift deserves.

Your next step is to let the Holy Spirit lead you to a local church where you can serve God, learn the Word, and pass it on to others to do the job Jesus wants you to do.

If someone prayed with you to receive baptism, ask him or her for guidance. Go to the church of your youth if you have one, or look in the phone book for a full-gospel church; that's a Christian code word for a church that believes in the present-day gifts of the Holy Spirit.

(End of tract)

Some people will receive a more enthusiastic outpouring of tongues than others will, but all who earnestly ask will receive. Jesus said so, so that makes it fact. The next step is to encourage each person you pray with or exhort about baptism and encourage him or her to pray daily in tongues.

Newly baptized believers need to develop their confidence and faith and speak out in tongues daily. Use the example of "confess with your mouth and believe in your heart that Jesus is Lord" (Romans 10:10). To evidence salvation, you need to confess Jesus is your Lord. To evidence baptism in the Holy Spirit, you need to speak in tongues. Both are acts of faith. Encourage them to pray in tongues in their private time, commune with God, and grow in Christ. Encourage them to read the tract and look up the scriptures. Get them into the Word!

If they mention that they are in a church that opposes Spirit-filled people, you have a delicate issue to overcome. The Bible is your resource; quote it often, but don't criticize the denomination or the clergy with an opposing opinion. Never criticize God's anointed. Just repeat the Word, preach the Word, and let God and the Holy Spirit do the convicting and the convincing.

Lead them tenderly and lovingly to a place where they can be sensitive to the leading of the Spirit, and let Him lead them to the place where they should be. Avoid the temptation to get them immediately involved in your church. If they are unchurched and have no preference, by all means bring them to your church. Move slowly, give support and comfort, but do not proselytize from another Christian church.

To stay on track, they need fellowship with other Spirit-filled believers; offer that support, but let the Spirit decide whether to move them from another church. He may have a work for them to do there. Don't play God.

Keep Galatians 1:8 in mind, and have new believers underline it in their Bibles. If anyone, even an angel, preaches a gospel different from what the apostles preached, let him or her be accursed. Those are strong words of condemnation, but the Bible said it. The newly baptized will have to discover truth for themselves. They will learn that those who preach against baptism in the Holy Spirit or against anything else the apostles preached are wrong. It is not for us to talk against another church or denomination; we are just to preach Jesus and Him risen.

Study lesson 5 for next week, and please read Deuteronomy 28.

LESSON 5

Healing

Everyone taking this training has to understand two absolutes; they aren't up for negotiation or discussion. If you cannot adhere to these two rules, please leave the program now.

1. NEVER advise others to stop seeing their doctors or following their medical advice. This goes for their children as well.

2. NEVER advise others to stop taking medications they are taking on the advice of their doctors. This goes for their children as well.

In John 2:23, many believed in Jesus because of the miracles He performed. In John 14:11, Jesus asked us to believe in Him and claimed He was God and God was in Him; believe this for the works' (miracles') sake. The scripture important to our studies in this lesson, verse 13, "Whatsoever you ask in my name that will I do that the Father may be glorified in the son"; keep going … verse 14: "If you ask anything in my name I will do it."

We are charged with praying for the sick in James 5:14. In 1 Peter 2:24 and Isaiah 53:5, we learn that Jesus bore our sins in His own body and by His stripes we were (past tense) healed.

In this introduction, we want to start building the confidence in you that you do have the right and the privilege to pray with the sick for healing. God has the responsibility to heal, not you. Let's go into this tract and begin our lesson. This tract was written so it could be used by a person who found it and had no Bible training. It can also be used as a reference for mature Christians as they witness to and pray for the sick. The tract is on the next page.

Healing Is for today

To be healed, we must believe in faith that what God says is truth all the time every time. What life's experiences or religion teaches us may be false. What God says in the Bible is truth, and we need to believe in faith what God says about healing and health. We must reject our life experiences and religious teachings that are contrary to God's Word. Even stronger than that, by holding on to this unbelief, we are in effect calling God a liar! When we reject God's Word, we also reject the blessings and promises in it.

Next, know where sickness came from. When Adam and Eve sinned against God and gave up the earth to Satan, sickness and death started. God explained this in Genesis 3, when Adam and Eve lost the protection of God in the garden and were driven out. The devil then had the lease on earth. Adam had given up the dominion God had given him; to this day, Satan has dominion over earth.

In John 10:10, Jesus told us that the devil came to steal, kill, and destroy. It is apparent that he has done a great job these thousands of years! But praise God, the second part of John 10:10 says, "I (Jesus) have come that they (meaning you and me) may have life, and life more abundantly." You don't have to have your health and happiness stolen, and you need not be killed by disease because you are promised the abundant life by Jesus Himself!

The Bible tells us that God is not a liar (Numbers 23:19; Titus 1:2; Hebrews 6:18). He said He was the God who healed us (Exodus 15:26). There has not failed one word of His good promise (1 Kings 8:56). He will hasten His Word to perform it (Jeremiah 1:12). God is not a respecter of persons (Acts 10:34), so since He healed others at other times, He will heal you now! Psalm 119:89 says, "Forever Lord your Word is settled in Heaven." That means past, present, and future—forever.

Jesus taught us how to pray the Lord's Prayer in Matthew 6:10; remember these words: "thy will be done on earth as it is in heaven." In John 3:2, we read, "Beloved (that's you and me) I wish above all things that you prosper and be in health even as your soul prospers."

Jesus bore our sicknesses when He was beaten before and during His crucifixion; 1 Peter 2:24 says by His stripes (beatings) we were healed. So it is already done! Believe the Bible, not what your experience, your feelings, or your religion teaches you if it doesn't line up with God's Word. If any statement, teaching, or belief is counter to God's Word, it's wrong and should be rejected as a lie. Healing is for today, for now; claim it in the name of Jesus. He wants you to be well.

In John 6:38, Jesus said, "I came down from Heaven not to mine own will, but in Him that sent me." The healing miracles that Jesus did were God's will in action. Nothing in the Bible suggests that God's will changed just because Jesus and the original apostles are no longer in their mortal bodies. In Hebrews 13:8, we are told that Jesus is the same yesterday, today, and forever. Jesus Himself ordered us believers to go out and preach the gospel. He told us to lay hands on the sick and they would recover. Did Jesus lie to us? Hardly. He never lied.

Read Mark 16:15–20; Jesus is talking to you here! Read John 14 carefully. Here, Jesus specifically promised the Holy Spirit and power even greater than He had. Also, note our obligations.

If you have just been prayed for, or had hands laid on you for healing, or if you are seeking healing, believe that you have just received it from Jesus; that's what God promised in the Bible. Don't believe your physical symptoms; they may exist, but they don't have a right to exist! Deny them the right to exist and cast them out in Jesus' name.

Continue taking your medicine if you have it, and follow your doctor's advice until your healing is confirmed by your doctor and he or she takes you off your medication. If your doctor exclaims, "I cannot understand how you were healed so quickly. It's a miracle," that's the best witness of all. Tell your doctor about Jesus; take a great opportunity to be a witness for Jesus. Pray continually until all your symptoms are gone.

Remember, Jesus had to pray twice for a blind man to receive his healing, so don't feel bad or lose faith just because you have to pray a number of times before your healing is seen and felt.

Here is a prayer for healing. Just insert the sickness or condition in the blank space.

"Dear God, I come to you as a born-again believer in Jesus Christ. I claim Him as my personal Lord and Savior. I believe you raised Him from the dead and He sits at your right hand in heaven. In his name, I believe I receive healing for ____ (say the sickness or condition attacking you here) that is attacking my body. I declare it a trespasser and cast out the spirit that is causing this condition now!

"My body is the temple of the Holy Spirit, and I will not have it defiled with sickness. By Jesus' stripes, I was healed. I am healed now because Jesus is the same yesterday, today, and forever. Thank you, God, for the promises in your Word. I will walk in faith. I forgive those I may be mad at or have something against. Thank you for my healing. I praise you for that, and I will thank you until all symptoms disappear. Then I will thank you that it is done. I will tell someone what Jesus did for me. In His name I pray, amen."

Next, get into a church where you hear preaching about God's healing power. Find a place where they openly lay hands on people and expect God's Word to be done. If you surround yourself with people who believe and act on God's Word, you'll be much better able to receive and keep your healing. If religious practice, unbelief, or tradition in a church teaches that the gifts of the Spirit such as healing are not for today, healing might not happen. Jesus Himself was prevented from doing great miracles in His hometown because they refused to believe in Him (Matthew 13:53–58). If a church doesn't believe, its members probably won't receive all God has for them.

Read what God has to say about folks like this in Galatians 1:8. It's impossible to improve on Paul's message from God on the subject of preaching of a compromised or incomplete gospel.

LESSON 6

Deliverance

In John 10:10, Jesus told us the devil came to _____, but (Jesus) came (and provided the Holy Spirit) so we_____ (my paraphrase).

Since the devil is not a human being but a spirit being, the only way he can harm anyone is by spiritual means. The ministry of deliverance seeks to drive these spirits away from those they are influencing or controlling.

In John 6:38, Jesus said, "I came down from Heaven not to mine own will, but in Him that sent me." The deliverance miracles Jesus performed were God's will in action. Jesus said we would do greater works in His name than even He did. Read John 14:12. It's unfortunate that arguments over whether Christians can be possessed by devils or oppressed by spirits have taken precedence over the ministry that gets rid of them. Some would rather argue semantics than deliver ministry to those in need!

In this segment of the exhorter training, we will give you a very basic overview of what deliverance is all about and get you to a place where you can pray with a person for deliverance and in faith expect it will happen. Please read the lesson and study the Bible verses. In the next meeting, everyone will be expected to share his or her experiences or inexperience of deliverance.

Remember that deliverance is a part of praying for many needs. We have all heard of spirits of illness and fear getting in the way of a Christian's walk with Jesus. We pray for these things all the time. Now, we're going to do a brief study of it so you can become better equipped to do what God puts in your path to do.

In biblical times, various populations worshipped many gods. The same is true today in parts of the world where voodoo and other forms of occult are practiced. There were even household gods just for single families. After the Christian reformation, many former *worshipers of multiple gods substituted angels or later saints as persons to pray to. These populations believed in a spirit world as a normal thing. In the Caribbean and Africa today, many people believe in the spirit world as a normal, everyday thing.

Modern Americans (Westerners) are not taught of the spirit world. Some may have academic knowledge that God is a Spirit and that there is a Holy Spirit; they probably have heard of voodoo, and nearly everyone has heard of Satan. But grasping the fact that there is a spirit world running along with our temporal world is a hard concept to understand for today's sophisticated and educated people.

So the negative influence of spirits under the command of Satan is either denied or ignored by many Christians. Their denominations have not taught them about spiritual warfare. You hear, "This went out when the disciples died off." Some excuse the influence of demon spirits as psychological defects or mental illness. Some churches just skip over any text that could be controversial. Others may even teach that deliverance is some kind of occult counterfeit of Christianity. Wow! How wrong can they be? It is a fact that Ephesians 6:12 is inoperative in some churches: "We war not against flesh and blood (people), but against the rulers, against the authorities, against the powers of this dark world, and against the spiritual forces of evil in the heavenly realms." In verse 18, after some instructions about the full armor of God, the Word says, "Pray in the spirit on all occasions with all kinds of prayers and requests."

In this church, we believe in the Word of God we read about in the Bible. Driving out spirits is a biblical mandate for us all. In Acts 5:15, we read that the early Christians prayed and healed the sick and drove out evil spirits. Nothing in the Bible suggests we are to do any differently today.

This is clearly a spiritual warfare situation, not a matter of taking up physical arms against a human foe. As we said in our last lesson, believe what the Bible says, not what your experience, feelings, or religion teaches you if it doesn't line up with God's Word. If any statement, teaching, or belief is counter to God's Word, it is wrong and should be rejected as a lie. Deliverance, like healing and salvation, *is* for today.

As Christian workers, we will be asked many questions about the Bible. We will not know all the answers, so we must exhort the questioner to read the Bible and discover the answers. This is not a cop-out; we must be diligent and lovingly guide them to the portions of the Bible (in context) that provide the answer. Knowing how to use a concordance and Bible dictionary are helpful skills.

One big question will be, "Can a Christian be demon possessed?" The short answer is no. Possession is having total ownership and total control. As Christians, we belong to God, so Satan cannot gain total control over us—end of story. Can non-Christians yield total control? Most likely. In Mark 1:23, Jesus encountered a man "possessed" by a spirit and cast it out. Examples in the Bible of people possessed by demons are not born-again Christians.

However, our advice is to avoid getting tangled in a discussion of semantics. Arguing if a condition or situation is possession, oppression, undue influence, or any other word for messing with our lives, health, and happiness is useless chatter whether the person in trouble is a Christian or an unsaved person. We can cast out the spirit. It makes no difference if the spirit oppressed them or possessed them. No matter whether it's inside them, next to them, on them, or whispering in their ear, none of these semantics issues makes any difference. If we cast it out, the problem is solved.

Modern scholars are substituting the word *demonized*, a transliteration of the Greek word *daimonizomai*, which had been translated as "demon possession" in early translations of the Bible. Using this substitute word avoids the inevitable arguments about possession, oppression, etc. What *is* possible is for Christians to yield some control over themselves to demon spirits in much the same way they could yield to a sin such as alcoholism or drug addiction.

Proof of this is when Paul warned us in Ephesians 4:27 not to give the devil a foothold. Paul wouldn't have preached about it if it were not possible for demons to cause us problems. This admonition is to not to let demonic spirits into our "space" if you will. "Foothold" in Greek means inhabitable space, like a room in your house. So we must guard our space, our minds, emotions, and fleshly tendencies against the spirits noted in Ephesians 6. Christians can give him a foothold. How many Christians have we known who committed adultery, went to jail for a crime, or did something else that gave glory to the devil and not to God?

In Job 1:6–8, Satan was described as a fallen angel (one of the sons of God) who roamed the earth and had power over things on it. Revelation 12:9 informs us that in earlier history (pre-Adam), the devil and his angels were cast out of heaven to earth. Jesus described it vividly in Luke 10:18; He actually saw Satan cast down to the earth like lightning. Satan and his spirits are still here! Deliverance is the method we use to get him away from Christians and others so the overcoming life can be enjoyed by all.

Because of Adam's fall, we are born sinners and have to receive salvation at some point in our lives to be saved from eternal damnation. We live in a sinful world (duh). It's sinful because the devil is the (little g) god of it. We can overcome the devil by the power of the Holy Spirit promised us by Jesus Christ.

Our goal is to disciple each other and live in Christian community with each other. When needed, we are to cast out spirits or demons that are causing trouble. Therefore, in answer to this possession/oppression question or one like it, explain as follows: Satan is called the god of this world (little g) in 2 Corinthians 4:4. We are temporary residents here on earth until we get to go to heaven and be with Jesus. While we are here, Satan's demonic spirits will seek to do his work of stealing, killing, and destroying Christians (and others).

Without getting into the semantics of possession, oppression, etc., you can guide the discussion to getting down to solving their problem. In Matthew 16:18, Christ said that on this rock (the Holy Spirit) He would build His church and the gates of hell would not prevail against it. We have the power because Jesus gave it to us. James 4:7 tells us we are to submit ourselves to God, resist the devil, and he will (not may) flee from you.

You cannot see Satan; he is a spirit as are his cohorts, the fallen angels. They must work in the spirit realm to cause things to happen in the temporal realm. Hence, they work on our minds and our fleshly instincts tempting us, beguiling us, and propagandizing us with sinful music and entertainment. Revelation 16:14 tells us that in the last days, spirits of demons will inhabit world leaders. They will try to inhabit you now, but they cannot. In Colossians 2:15, Jesus spoiled principalities and powers; He made a show of them openly, triumphing over them. He defeated them. He gave you power in the Holy Spirit so you could win.

However, as long as we live on earth, we will have to wage battle with Satan and his evil spirits. Let's move on and get into a place where we are comfortable with our rights and privileges in Jesus Christ, a place where we can confidently pray with someone and cast out evil spirits that are interfering with our lives.

One of the principal ways Satan can gain foothold is the mind, the imagination. Through suggestion, literature, listening to gossip, sinful entertainment, etc., he can exert control a little bit at a time. He doesn't need to possess anyone; he needs to exert only enough control to get you out of God's will and into self. Then, when he gets Christ out of your thoughts, he wins. It makes no difference if you get into sinful activities or just go overboard on physical fitness; once your mind is off Christ, the devil wins.

In Philippians 4:6, Paul said we need not be anxious about things but by prayer and petition and in thanks bring our requests to God. When we do, the peace that passes all understanding will guard our hearts and minds in Christ Jesus. In verse 8, Paul admonished us to think on things that are true, honest, just, pure, lovely—things of good report. Don't be bugged about negative things; think on God's Word and His blessings, and guard your mind. To the extent that you do, the devil cannot get a foothold.

These are points we have to get across to those we pray with. This deliverance session is not a one-time event; it's a process that begins with the binding and casting out of the spirit. Then we go to Romans 12:2: "Be not conformed to this world but be transformed by the renewing of your MIND." Look also at 2 Corinthians 10:4: "The weapons of our warfare are not carnal or worldly, but mighty through Divine power to bring down strongholds."

Exhort those you pray with that good things must go in their minds through their eyes and ears, and good things must come out of their mouths. It's the divine GIGO concept—garbage in garbage out, or in God's terms, good in, good out. Jesus explained this in Luke 6:45.

In Corinthians 1:5, we read, "We take captive every thought to make it obedient to Christ." Those we pray with must see that the process is a renewing of their minds and a change in their way of life to conform to a godly instead of a worldly example. Reading the Bible and seeking God's answers will give them peace.

We can bind and cast out spirits, but the job is not done. We must assure ourselves that those we pray with are sincere in wanting the spirits out. Next, they will have to commit to a different lifestyle, one that denies spirits a place (room in the house) to exist. Then we need to see to it that there is follow-up to disciple them in the Word. Get them in a church or Bible study; they need to fill themselves with God things; that will fill the void left by the evil spirits and the inappropriate behavior that previously inhabited their minds or bodies.

Jesus is clear what will happen if people aren't committed to getting rid of the evil spirits and insincere when they pray. Read Mark 11:24. Wow! If we jump to pray a spirit out of a person, if the timing is not right, if instruction in righteousness is not given and received, then seven worse spirits can enter the person, and they will be worse than before! This is not my opinion; that is the Word of Christ.

The ministry of deliverance is a duty of all of us. Mark 16:17 admonishes us to go out, witness Jesus Christ, and cast out demons. But having the power and duty is like having the keys to a car and not knowing how to drive. We have studied the topic of deliverance; now let's get down to some practicalities.

Are you truly mature in your walk with Christ? Are you practicing a godly life as best you can? Do you read and study your Bible regularly? Do godly things mean more to you than worldly things? Look at your calendar and checkbook; are a significant part of your time and resources spent on God? Do you feel secure in your walk with Jesus? Can you witness without timidity and continue praying without making excuses when prayers are not immediately answered?

Are you free of habits that don't glorify God? Habits like smoking, drinking, drugs, pornography, lust, bad spending habits, failure to discipline children, marital discord, financial irresponsibility, etc. We must clean ourselves up before trying to clean others. Our code of conduct is a benchmark we all must conform to in this church.

Next, before praying for someone, be prayed up yourself. I heard one preacher say that he prayed in the Spirit for a number of hours before ever ministering. Jesus explained this to the disciples in Mark 9:29; He clearly stated that being prayed up was required to harness the power to cast out some devils. If Jesus had to stay prayed up, we sure do! We need to know we're ready to engage in spiritual warfare.

We all live every day in a temporal world; we drive, we eat, we see things and people. We do not regularly confront spirits. When we're planning on fighting one (or more), we better be prayed up and operating in a spiritual state, not a natural state. Instead of listening to oldies on the radio, have a praise tape or a study tape on in the car. Keep the good things going in your eyes and ears so you will be ready to act when needed. In 2 Timothy 4:2, we are told to be ready in and out of season.

Jesus quickly discerned evil spirits and cast them out. We need to be operating in the Spirit so we can identify them if needed and cast them out if appropriate at that time. We have to discern the motives of the person, the attitude, the commitment to a changed life, and discern the spirit—a big job for a truck driver or an office worker but perhaps easier for a carpenter!

If you have time, you should do the same thing the intercessory prayer people do every Sunday at the church. Pray over the place you are meeting, and cast out any spirits that would interfere with God's work. Pray for an anointing on yourself and anyone assisting you. If someone is available to intercede for you during the session, that's a plus. We make this same duty normal for ushers during a prayer service; they always intercede for the people at the altar.

Some churches have a team of three praying for the service in another room during the service. You can arrange for this if you know you're going to be praying for someone; have two or three people praying for you at home just to gird you up during the deliverance session.

The last item in preparation is a firm belief in your mind that you have the right and the power (2 Corinthians 10:4) to do what is needed in the situation that is causing the person problems. If you are timid or unsure of yourself, get some help. Matthew 18:19 tells us, "Where 2 agree about anything you ask for, it will be done for you by My Father in Heaven." Jesus advises that two are better than one.

Let's review.

1. You are in good spiritual condition.
2. You are prayed up, ask for discerning of spirits.
3. You believe you will receive from Christ through the Holy Spirit the direction to pray for the person in need.
4. You have someone interceding for you and the situation.

Your best tools in a session of deliverance are your ears. Listen to those you are praying with. Get them talking about the situation. There may be biblical answers to a problem that has nothing to do with an evil spirit. Exhort them with appropriate Bible scriptures that address the situation—scriptures on marriage, on money, on raising kids, etc.

Or they may be involved in dumb conduct that is obvious without any spiritual discernment at all—drinking, drugs, etc. Some may be making bad judgements. Yes, they may be assisted by satanic spirits, but not necessarily. As God's creations, we have free will. Some people do dumb things by their dumb will, not by spiritual influence. Satan wins in these cases, and he doesn't even have to put forth any effort!

If you discern that it is a spiritual problem, share your reasons with those you are praying with. Get them talking again; wait for the Holy Spirit to reveal to you the way to pray. They may reveal something obvious; perhaps they are involved in some occult activity or have an addiction. Before praying the offending spirit out, make sure the person is truly repentant of his or her sin, committed to a lifestyle change, and is agreeable to be prayed for. Inform him or her that backsliding could multiply the problem by a factor of seven.

This is not fast-food Christianity—a quick prayer and get on with life. This calls for a serious commitment on the part of the person desiring prayer. If you discern he or she is ready, pray with him or her.

First, solidify salvation, take them through the sinner's prayer (whichever one you use) so you both know that they are saved. Make sure they are not harboring unforgiveness even for themselves. Matthew 6:14 tells us that if we don't forgive others, God won't forgive us. Mark 11:25 tells us that we cannot harbor unforgiveness and expect forgiveness from God. People hating themselves for transgressions of the past is common and must be dealt with before deliverance.

Next, anoint them with oil if you have it and cast out the offending, trespassing, evil spirit forever! Speak to the spirit in authority and cast it out the way you would throw out a trespasser or burglar from your home. Get out!

Next, attempt to lead them in baptism in the Holy Spirit. If they can receive this gift in faith and begin to speak in tongues, they have a large part of their battle won already. Evil spirits cannot be in the same place as the Holy Spirit. If they are baptized in the Holy Spirit, that will enable them to pray in the Spirit and edify themselves and build their faith to continue to battle the devil from coming back after deliverance.

To sum up, we have learned some important facts.

1. There is a spirit world.
2. Jesus gave us the gifts of the Holy Spirit including the discerning of spirits for a reason—to use them.
3. Spirits can cause people problems; the unsaved can even be possessed totally by them. The saved cannot be possessed, but they can be negatively influenced by them.
4. We need to be living good, Christian lives and be prayed up to be prepared for the task of praying out spirits.
5. We need to disciple, to assist those we pray with so they will not backslide and get seven times more problems.

Homework: Read ahead in lesson 8 and look up the scriptures. Bring in a question that will interest others.

LESSONS 7 AND 8

Motivational Gifts I

Welcome to the next two weeks of fun and intense study.

The gifts that will be the subject of the next two meetings are those you read at home this week in Romans 12:2–7, commonly called the motivational or foundational gifts. They could also be called personality gifts. How we move in our gifts is how others perceive us and to an extent how we perceive ourselves.

How others move in their gifts will influence how we witness to them or work with them as fellow Helps workers. Remember Romans 12:2—each according to the measure of faith God apportioned. During these next two weeks, you will see why we advised you to review lessons 3 through 6; they are the basis for how we study the motivational gifts.

Secular psychologists and salesmanship teachers have other names for these personality types—what Christians call motivational gifts mentioned in the Bible versus categories assigned by science or the business world. They are the attitudes and motivations we naturally operate with. How we approach and solve problems, how we interact with people, and the occupation or profession we choose will be greatly influenced by the God-given gift that is primary in our lives.

Most agree that we are all combinations of gifts. One, however, will stand out, and we call that our primary gift. Our objective in this class is to acquaint you with the gifts, discuss them briefly, and contrast them with other gifts mentioned in the Bible. As Christians, we should know what our gift is and be able to recognize others' gifts so we can be more effective in witnessing to them and teaching them.

A study of the motivational gifts must begin with a short overview of other gifts so confusion will not occur about gifts with similar names. Hopefully, you have read all these scripture references. Before we start, are there any questions about the different gift categories?

(Instructor: handle any questions now.)

We do not have time to go over them all thoroughly in class; we trust you did your homework and studied them at home. However, we can hit the high spots. You may see a gift that has the same name in Romans 12 with a ministerial gift in Ephesians 4 and with the Holy Spirit gifts in 1 Corinthians 12. We will see similar terms used, but the meanings are different.

First let's turn to Ephesians 4:11: "And He Himself gave some to be apostles, some prophets, some evangelists, and some pastors and teachers." Let's review them. You should have read these, so we will move quickly.

Apostle

This means **one sent** such as a missionary or a church planter, people sent from place to place with a charge from the church to accomplish a task. This is usually to start a new work, raise up leadership, and move on. The Greek word is *apostolos*.

Prophet

A prophet is a divine philosopher who points to the **future** or **past** and makes a point or **takes a stand** for God. Moses was one. The Greek word is *prophetes*.

Evangelist

An evangelist stirs things up and attracts others by **performing miracles**. An evangelist brings **glad tidings** as compared with the prophet, who may not do that. The Greek word is *euangelistes*.

Pastor

The Greek word is *poimen*; it was translated **pastor** once and **shepherd** sixteen times in the New Testament. In Hebrew, it is *ra'ha*; it was translated as *pastor* eight times and as *shepherd* sixty-three times in the Old Testament.

Teacher

This is a teachers of **truth** in the churches. The Greek word is *didaskalos*.

These are commonly referred to as the fivefold ministry gifts and are terms associated with people who hold offices in vocational ministry. They are ordained or licensed people who have answered the call to leadership in the church.

The next grouping of gifts are the Holy Spirit gifts given to all Christians who ask for them. These are sometimes called the charismatic gifts. You should see these gifts in operation in a Charismatic or Pentecostal church service. These are not offices as are the fivefold ministry gifts; rather, they are power gifts promised to Christians by Jesus. They fall in three groupings; you found these in 1 Corinthians 12 starting at verse 8.

First are the three revelation gifts or soul gifts.

- word of knowledge (v. 8)
- word of wisdom (v. 8)
- discerning of spirits (v. 10)

Next, the power gifts or body gifts.

- faith (v. 9)
- working of miracles (v. 10)
- healings of all kinds (v. 9)

Finally, the spoken or Spirit gifts.

- diverse tongues—public or private (v. 10)
- interpretation of tongues—usually public (v. 10)
- prophesy (v. 10)

These are the gifts referred to when someone exclaims that the congregation moved in the Spirit or moved in body life. The Corinthians were misusing these gifts, so Paul had to instruct them in 1 Corinthians 12–14.

With that short introduction, let's move to the motivational, foundational, or personality gifts, whatever you choose to call them. Hopefully, everyone marked Romans 12 in their Bibles, so let's start at verse 3.

(This teaching was inspired by a class I had in Bible school presented wonderfully by Marilyn Hickey. I have used her examples since they are so clear and to the point. For anything good about the next two classes, thank God and Marilyn. These are the gifts.)

Prophesy

This person likes to identify motives. They are very direct, and things are usually seen as black or white. Draw an eye. (Greek *propheteia*)

Ministry

Does practical needs—janitor, cook, carpenter, audiovisual, etc.; a helper type. Draw a hand. (Greek *diakona*)

Teacher

Teachers are very into the Word; everything is Word this and Word that. They hear the Word and have to tell everyone about it. Draw an ear. (Greek *didascein*, to give instruction)

Exhortation

This type of person loves to help people through situations, give spiritual advice, and encourage spiritual growth; they love people. They are always there, like a tree. Draw a tree. (Greek *parakalein*)

Giving

Those with this gift love to give; they share generously with others and like to involve others in giving. Draw a dollar sign. (Greek *metadidomi*)

Organizing

Also known as "ruler" in the KJV. They set goals and motivate others to attain those goals. Draw a head. (Greek *postemi*)

Mercy

Identifies emotional needs and wounds and tries to patch them up. Draw a heart for this one. (Greek *eleeo*)

Now that we have all the gifts listed and have our little memory-jogging pictures, let's begin by filling in the blanks with more-detailed explanations of these gifts to identify ourselves and some of our brothers and sisters. This is particularly important if we have had difficulty understanding just where others are coming from. Perhaps we can receive some revelation and have an easier time relating to others in the body and witnessing to people too.

Someone who may have an entirely different motivational gift than you do will approach a task in a vastly different way than you do. Hopefully, these two classes will give you a perspective on how to get along better. Another thing that can irritate any of us is when we rate something as having a higher importance than someone else does. We cannot for the life of us believe others don't have the same passion for an idea that we do. These two classes will get you on track to figure this out. Knowing your and others' motivational gifts can avoid confrontations and disagreements and foster cooperation. Many Christians have mistaken the actions of others working innocently and diligently in their gifts as direct insults to them, who have different motivational gifts. We will illustrate some examples of potential conflicts as the discussion moves on.

Many times, we have all marveled when a Christian believer effectively witnesses to someone after our attempts at that had failed. In many cases, that Christian was able to recognize where the person was coming from and used a different approach. Let's use God's Word to learn how we can be better witnesses and better supervisors of other Helps workers.

Let us use an imaginary volunteer work program at a church for our example and discussion. This is in your workbook, and hopefully, you will see yourself or someone else in the examples. Any comments?

(If everyone reports having read the "First Church" at home, use it for starting the discussion and skip to the next page and summarize.)

The name of this mythical church is:

The Highly Religious Church of Miscommunication

We will discuss some real Helps workers and see where things are going right and wrong. The first couple of weeks, this church had its volunteer worker program and everything went okay, but then, interest waned. By the end of the first month, there weren't enough workers left to get the jobs done on time.

We will pretend to listen in on volunteers planning how to get others in the church to join their efforts in getting things back on track. Hopefully, this imaginary conversation will illustrate how saints with differing motivational gifts approach the same challenge.

Pete the Prophet jumps up, waves his arms, and declares, "We need to contact every one of the people who signed up to work and confront them with their lack of responsibility to God's work. Since they didn't do the work they promised to do, they should be removed from the ministry."

Manny the Minister says, "Wait. If we all just work a little harder, we can get it done." He works all night on the project.

Tom the Teacher says, "That might work. The Word says we can do all things through Christ. However, the Word also says those who don't work don't get to eat. So why should we do their share of the work?"

Eric the Exhorter decides to drop by shirkers' homes and tell them how much they are missed, how rewarding the work is, and how important to the kingdom it is. He proposes to uplift and encourage them back into the group.

Greg the Giver suggests, "Let's take up a special offering to have the job done professionally." He seeds $100 as an encouragement for others to join in the effort.

Oliver the Organizer laments that if he had been in charge from the first, he would have had a second and possibly a third backup group. "There should have been a schedule of when and where to report and what needed to be done. Further, a phone notification would have reminded and encouraged people to show up. And last, if there was a problem, I would have had backups or a professional in place to get the job done."

Martin the Merciful says, "Let's calm down. We need to figure out why the folks didn't show up. Perhaps there was sickness in the family we need to pray about. These are good people. I'm sure they just forgot. Let's not be judgmental."

(Instructor: begin again here.)

Perhaps this is an exaggerated example of how some people in the seven motivational types might react to the same problem. A variation on this has probably happened in every church any of us has attended. We see varying reactions from people who live in certain gifts. Does anyone want to venture a guess of which one was right?

They perceived this lack of participation in vastly differing ways. Though none knew for sure why the people didn't show up, they all had a solution. Any of the solutions could be correct for someone but would be grossly inappropriate for others.

Can we see how easy it would be for Pete the Prophet to feel that Martin the Merciful was too soft or that all Tom the Teacher did was spout the Word and never got anything practical done? Pete the Prophet witnessed salvation too aggressively and did not motivate Martin to make a decision. Eric the Exhorter may have thought Pete the Prophet was just a frustrated first sergeant always pushing his weight around, and they all might have considered Oliver the Organizer lazy. He just wrote stuff down and never wanted to get his hands dirty. Gilbert the Giver might have been in for some flak because he wasn't in the thick of the work either. What they don't see is that he needs to work more hours to generate the extra money he was giving.

Tom the Teacher might have quietly looked at the whole bunch and thought, *If they were all in the Word enough, God would supply the answer.* Manny the Minister thought, *If these people would quit discussing things and get to work, we could get this job done before midnight.*

You can see how we could carry out these examples to include all seven and really have some arguments. Perhaps in your church life, you have experienced some of these frustrations and the resulting hurt feelings. But once you have finished these two lessons, you will have a greater appreciation for the differing gifts and develop the ability to effectively work with others who have different motivation gifts. The basic objective of this entire course is to win souls to Christ. The unsaved have these same motivations, so knowing them and appreciating them will make you a more effective witness of the gospel.

Pastors and ministry leaders must know the motivations of those working for them so duties and responsibilities can be assigned correctly and effectively. That is part of why we take two weeks on this topic and why it is integrated in lessons 3 through 6. That gives you more opportunity to hone your skills and the leadership more opportunity to assist you.

In studying these next two weeks, we hope the message of sensitivity and tolerance has been communicated. You still may not like that Gilbert gives bucks and never gets his hands dirty. You still may have a tinge of criticism for Tom, who stays home to study his next lesson and doesn't show up for work details. You also may still wonder why someone with a different ministry gift easily wins others to Christ when our efforts have failed. But now, we won't worry about it too much. Let's take joy in the fact God made us all different, not all hands or feet or heads. We all have our places in the body of Christ.

(Instructor: this intro is for after lesson 7 to prepare them for lesson 8.)

Introduction for Lesson 8

Next week, we begin the study of faithfulness, specifically, the kind of faithfulness that is exhibited by the following.

- being on time to work
- doing a good job
- finishing on time
- keeping our word
- helping others
- and more

The fill-ins for next week are a challenge. Glean the name in scripture of the person or the attribute the scripture defines. It's not easy, but have fun.

Please do the homework; that's an important part of the program. You will find it interesting how many times God's Word gives us practical examples of people who were faithful to their duties. It will be an inspiration to us in our church work and on our jobs.

In your workbook is a handout with some scripture references on it. Your assignment is to look them up and make appropriate notes for each one. Next week, we will discuss them in class, and we'll all have opportunities to share our answers to one or more of the questions.

(Instructor: here is a list of the gifts printed in longer form at the end of the student's workbook.)

Prophecy

A person who tells you how evil everyone is and knocks the body of Christ by trying to show off his or her authority is not motivated by the gift of prophecy.

The prophecy motive affects others five ways.

1. bringing people to accountability by exposing their motives
2. revealing their hearts' motivations
3. causing an inner conviction
4. bringing an awareness of God's presence
5. making people fall on their knees when repentance is necessary

Here are the characteristics of the person with the prophecy motive gift:

- They have a need to express the message verbally. It burns in their hearts and must be expressed aloud.

- They have insight and ability to easily discern the characters and motives of other people.

- They possess a divine capacity to identify, define, and hate evil. They come down hard on evil and sin. If they see others being dragged down into sin, they will be sure to tell them about it.

- They are willing to experience brokenness to prompt brokenness and draw the same emotion out of other people.

- Their authority is always based on scripture, not their own authority.

- They desire outward evidence that demonstrates inner conviction. They want to see outward evidence of people repenting. They will do all they can to get people to confess before God and break through to victory.

- They are direct, frank, and persuasive in speaking. They are extremely honest. They will look you in the eye and give you the truth about your situation.

- They are concerned for the reputation and program of God. They set forth standards of excellence that are in keeping with God's Word.

- When dealing with others, they experience personal identification and inner weeping for their sin. They are in love with those sinners they counsel, and their first concern is to see them escape the bondage of sin. They will identify so strongly with others that they will feel as though they were also involved in the sin.

- They are eager for others to point out their own blind spots. They don't just run around telling everyone else what's wrong with them. They are so direct and honest that they want to know if they themselves have blind areas. They are loving, not cruel in their dealing with others.

Now let's examine the misunderstanding of a prophecy motive:

- Their frankness may be viewed as harshness. Honesty can hurt, and that's why the truth must be spoken in love.

- Their interest in groups may be interpreted as disinterest in individuals. They often discern the body of Christ as a whole and may say, "This church needs more founding in the Word."

- Their efforts to obtain results may be seen as gimmicky. John the Baptist and Ezekiel were very gimmicky. Gimmicks are still used because they bring a visual aid lesson with the Word. Some people may think that isn't spiritual.

- Their focus on right and wrong may be judged as intolerance. They are so strong about the black and white that they are often accused of not giving credit for good in certain situations.

- Their emphasis on decisions may appear as neglecting spiritual growth. They concentrate on decisions and commitments rather than on individual growth.

- Their public boldness and strict standards may hinder personal relationships. They usually don't have many close friends because their discernment can repel people. They can come on very strong, and some people just can't take someone being in their faces.

- Their strong desire to convey truth may appear as a lack of interest in listening to another person's point of view.

Serving

Here are the characteristics of those with a serving motivational gift.

- Servers are able to recall specific likes and dislikes of people.

- They're alert to detect and meet practical needs. They see needs before most people even notice them.

- They are motivated to meet needs as quickly as possible. They don't like long-term goals; they'd rather get everything done immediately.

- They may be exhausted but will disregard that.

- They are willing to use personal funds rather than wait for the church board to approve something.

- They can sense sincere appreciation and detect insincerity. They know whether they're appreciated. They can detect phonies.

- They desire to complete jobs with evidence of unexpected extra service. They enjoy doing extra things that you never asked them for.

- Servers may be extremely involved due to their inability to say no. They are so caught up in offering service that it usually does not occur to them to draw any line.

- They enjoy reaching short-term goals; long-term goals tend to frustrate them because they don't see the overall picture, just the result.

- They dislike time limitations on jobs.

Here are the misunderstandings that may occur; there are many because servers are very apt to be misunderstood.

- Their quickness in meeting needs may seem to be pushiness.

- Their avoidance of red tape may exclude others from jobs someone else may have wanted to do.

- Their disregard for personal needs can create needs in their families.

- Their eagerness to serve may prompt suspicion of self-advancement or trying to get in good with the pastor, not their real motives.

- Servers may react when others don't detect and meet obvious needs. They can become unhappy when others don't share their motive of meeting others' needs.

- They have a very hard time accepting service. They are so busy with serving everyone else that they don't realize that on occasion, God wants them to allow others to serve them.

- Their desire for sincere appreciation may result in their being easily hurt.

- Their quickness in meeting needs may interfere with spiritual lessons for others. If a family in the church is experiencing financial pressure, they'll be over with food and money, but perhaps that family isn't tithing. God may want to tell such families that they won't be blessed until they begin to obey His Word.

- Their meeting practical needs may interfere with spiritual matters. Servers are so concerned that everyone is happy—they want the church and kitchen clean and the nursery running smoothly—but this may cause them to miss church services.

- Their stamina may be interpreted as insensitivity to others.

- Their enjoyment of short-range goals may result in disorganization of long-range objectives. They might paint the nursery without finding out that it was to be knocked out the next month.

- Their desire to get things done may result in sidetracking their employers' directions. They may get into things that are not necessary at all. They may run in and meet a need while the pastor is dealing with the overall situation and end up getting ahead of him.

Teaching

Here are the characteristics of a person with the teaching motivational gift.

- They believe that their gifts are foundational and that teaching God's Word must be the foundation of ministry.

- They place emphasis on the accuracy of words because they are so truth oriented.

- They tend to test the knowledge of those who teach them.

- They delight in research that validates truth. Studying the Word is the number-one priority of teaching. They find fulfillment in discovering new ways to establish God's precepts.

- They use established truth to validate new information.

- They present truth in systematic sequence.

- They avoid illustration from nonbiblical sources to maintain credibility.

- They resist scriptural illustrations out of context; that really turns them off.

- They find greater joy in researching truth than presenting it. They would rather study than present material even though they still enjoy the presentation. They are jealous about study time, for that is where they receive their fulfillment.

Now the misunderstandings.

- Their emphasis on accuracy of scriptural interpretation may seem to be a neglecting of its practical application. They can become so busy proving a point with accuracy that they don't apply it to their own lives.

- Their involvement with research can distract them from the Holy Spirit's teaching. They can delight in research so much that there is a danger in getting out of the Holy Spirit's teaching ministry and into the intellect.

- Their use of knowledge to test others may seem prideful. When teachers begin to say, "That person said so-and-so, and that's not scriptural," people tend to react by saying, "Who do you think you are?" Teachers tend to be quite picky about what people say if it isn't scripturally based.

- Their concern of imparting research details can seem unnecessary. They love detail and often expect others to share that feeling.

- Their need for objective research may appear to lack warmth. Sometimes, teachers can seem cold and analytical, and it may appear that they don't apply their teaching. They just want to get the truth out and may concentrate on that rather than the application.

Exhortation

The main thrust of an exhorter is people, whereas the main thrust of the teacher is truth. There is a strong contrast between the motive gifts of teaching and exhortation.

Here are the characteristics of exhorters.

- They desire to visualize specific achievements and prescribe precise steps of action. They want to give you steps on coming out of trials.

- They tend to avoid systems of information that lack practical application. If they can't see how something can be practically applied in someone's life, they tend to put that teaching on the shelf.

- Exhorters can see how tribulation can produce maturity. They look for positive benefits. They will use your trials to make something productive in your life.

- They are dependent on visible acceptance when speaking to groups or individuals because they are so concerned about people being able to apply their knowledge.

- They use insight from human experience to validate and apply scripture. They are always on the lookout for human experience that relate to the Word. A teacher will say Word first, experience second, but the exhorter will give experience first and then the Word.

- They enjoy counseling those who are eager to follow steps of action and are happy when someone responds to their steps. They are excited about people and enjoy seeing these steps bring forth positive benefits in their lives.

- They are grieved when teaching is not made practical. If they do not see an audience grasping the truth, they grieve on the inside.

- They delight in personal conferences. They love to counsel especially when they see the counselee taking hold of the Word and practicing it for results.

Here are the misunderstandings.

- Emphasis on steps of action may seem like oversimplification.

- Urgency in having plans may appear as overconfidence in them. Some people feel that exhorters place too much emphasis on the action rather than on the spiritual matter behind that action.

- Their desire to witness through being living examples can look like disinterest in evangelism.

- Using scripture for practical application may take it out of context. Exhorters are so concerned about making the Word flesh in your life that they may not follow the whole context through. This can really make others critical.

- Their emphasis on steps of action may appear to disregard the feelings of those being exhorted. Some say that these people get so carried away with their steps and plans that they can't recognize how others felt. Exhorters feel if you do steps 1–2–3–4–5, this will solve your problems.

Giving

True motivation givers do not use their gifts in an attempt to run the church or control the pastor.

Here are the characteristics of a person with the motivational gift of giver.

- They have the ability to make wise purchases and investments. They have natural talents in this regard and are motivated in it with their spiritual motive gift.

- They desire to give quietly to ministries and projects. They love to give, and they don't make a big splash about it.

- Givers will use their giving to motivate others to give. They want everyone to give, and they'll attempt to encourage others with their own giving. When they counsel someone with a problem, usually the first thing they'll ask is, "Do you tithe and give offerings?" They want others to be blessed through giving just as they themselves are.

- They're alert to valid needs that others may overlook. They also seek out needs that the church can give to.

- They enjoy meeting needs without the pressure of appeals. They are already motivated to give, so they don't need the pressure of appeals. Their motivation comes from the spiritual gift God has given them.

- They receive tremendous joy when their gifts are answers to specific prayers.

- Givers seem to use a witness back and forth for a confirmation of their gifts.

- Givers want their gift to be of high quality. They don't want to give any old thing. They're not giving to people; they are giving to Jesus.

- They want to feel they're part of the work done through their gifts.

Here are some insights on the misunderstandings of a giver.

- Their emphasis on money appears to be a focus on temporal values. When they have been blessed in their giving and testify about it, many people will criticize them, saying,

"All they ever think about is money." Givers are not focused on temporal things, but they are thrilled with the way God works in their life through giving. Giving can be a very spiritual thing, and there is much scripture about it.

- The desire of increasing the ministry's effectiveness may appear manipulative. People who attempt to manipulate ministries through gifts do not possess the motive gift of giving. This can be very dangerous and very enticing to a ministry in financial trouble by causing them to look to that person rather than to God.

- Personal frugality may be interpreted as selfishness. Sometimes, people with a strong motive to give don't live in high fashion. Many times, people who are motivated to give are very down to earth. Often, they are saving to give to the kingdom of God rather than spending money on themselves.

- Sometimes, they give so much their families suffer and do without.

Organization

Here are the characteristics of a person with the organizational motivational gift.

- They love to examine the overall picture, and their goals are set up accordingly.

- They organize only that for which they are responsible. You will not find this person trying to take over your job.

- They desire to complete tasks as quickly and efficiently as possible.

- They are aware of the resources available to complete tasks. You never see on organizer doing a project without first having all the necessary resources to complete it.

- They have an ability to know who can handle certain tasks. This is a spiritual insight that enables them to pick the right people for jobs.

- They tend to stand on the sidelines until responsibility is turned over to them. They will not jump in and grab the reigns without having been asked.

- They may assume responsibility if no structured leadership exists. If no one is there to supervise or lead, they will naturally assume the position of leadership.

- They are willing to endure reaction from workers in accomplishing tasks. They are motivated to rule and can take static from people because they have their minds on accomplishing the ultimate task. If an exhorter gets static from people, they might fall apart, but not a person with an organizational motive.

- They receive fulfillment in seeing the pieces come together and watching others enjoy the finished product. They are more turned on by seeing everyone else's excitement with the accomplishments than at what they have done themselves.

- They desire to move toward new challenges at the completion of tasks. They are not satisfied to do just one thing and then quit. It is their natural desire to go on to another challenge or else they may become bored. Their desire and challenge is that God's work be organized and that the people flow to meet challenges together.

Now the misunderstandings of an organizer motive.

- Their ability to delegate responsibility may seem to be an avoidance of work. They are not lazy; they just want to see others accomplishing with ease.

- Their willingness to endure reaction may appear to be callous. Someone may say, "He doesn't care what color I want for my classroom; he just went ahead and got the job done without asking." Organizers must be careful about this. These misunderstanding are areas where we want people to understand us.

- Neglect in task explanation may fail to stimulate response. This is probably the greatest misunderstanding of this gift. Sometimes, they say, "We're going to do this, and we need this many people," but they don't motivate people to volunteer to the positions. They are so highly motivated that they forget to express the same motivation that stimulates others.

- Their viewing of people as resources may place more emphasis on projects than on people. They are so turned on about goal accomplishment that they may wear out the people involved in driving them toward the result.

- Their desire to complete tasks swiftly may appear as insensitivity to others' priorities. Some people may not want to put in that much time and become unhappy with the organizer. They can really forget about the priorities of others because they are so caught up in reaching their goals.

Mercy

If you don't have the motive gift of mercy, remember that the Bible tells you to "put on the bowels of mercy."

Here are the characteristics of the person with the mercy gift,

- They possess ability to sense atmospheres of joy or distress in individuals and groups. They are very sensitive to peoples' feelings, reactions, and emotions.

- They are attracted to and understand people in distress. Their gift causes them to bring in stray people who are in trouble and need help. They will take sides with the underdog.

- Mercy motives desire to remove hurts and bring healing. They can't stand to see people who have been shattered. It almost shatters them, so they want to run and help by offering them mercy.

- They are more greatly concerned for mental rather than physical distress. They are really tuned on to people's mental afflictions and turmoil, so they are much more deeply concerned with mental and emotional rather than physical healing.

- They avoid firmness unless it will bring benefit to the wounded person. They can be firm but are sensitive about the timing.

- They're sensitive to words and actions that hurt others. They select their words and actions carefully because they don't want to hurt others. They are always concerned that someone will get trampled.

- They can discern sincere motives in others. They are not just soft individuals; they have a spiritual ability that discerns what is behind actions, and this discernment is similar to a prophecy motivation. Their reaction, however, is different.

- Merciful people enjoy uniting with others who are merciful; this is not so among those with other gifts. They enjoy talking about how they can show mercy and discern motivations.

- They tend to close their spirits to those who are insensitive. When someone will not come through and be sensitive to others but are calloused or insincere, mercy people have a cutoff point.

Mercy misunderstandings.

- They may seem weak or indecisive because they won't come down firmly on every situation. This may be perceived as being weak or indecisive.

- Their spiritual sensitivity may appear illogical, but they do not respond to people with their logical minds. A teaching motive is often critical of emotional response of mercy motivated people, but their motivation is spiritual, and they are led to show mercy.

- Attraction of those in distress may be misinterpreted by the opposite sex. This can be a danger. They could become involved in sexual situations, so they must learn where mercy has a stopping place especially when men have the mercy gift because women are romantically attracted to caring, understanding, merciful men.

- Sensitivity to harmful words and actions may appear that they take another's offense. Mercy is not to pick up others' offenses. If a person has been offended because they did right, the glory of God will rest upon them, but there is no glory for the person who picks up the offense. They must be careful to extend only God's mercy and not to take sides.

- They tend to be cautious with certain people because of their ability to detect insincerity. This may cause some people to find them "hard to get to know."

LESSON 9

Faithfulness

(Note to instructor: the faithfulness scriptures follow the text. The answers the attendees should have made will appear in **_bold italics_** in your copy.)

The objective of this lesson is to instill in the Helps worker a sense of what faithfulness and commitment are.

- to have them examine their hearts and determine if they are ready to make a serious commitment to Jesus Christ
- to make up their minds to manifest that commitment by becoming faithful and committed workers in their local congregations
- to submit to the leadership of their pastor as the representative of Jesus Christ in the local church
- to be viewed a person who has "sold out to Jesus." (If so, others in the church must see it in their actions.)

In this lesson, we will look at some definitions of faithfulness and commitment in the Word. We will learn that both are paths a person must decide to follow. We will discuss how it is a secure feeling to be committed and faithful to any number of ideas, people, family, spouses, branches of service, and of course the church you have chosen to belong to. You can perhaps think of other things people are committed to.

One outstanding example of faithfulness and commitment was demonstrated by the twelve disciples. They all worked for three years for the greatest evangelist ever. They traveled under harsh conditions sometimes. And except for a little tiff about who was going to sit by Jesus (Matthew 20:20–24), they gave the glory to Him and not to themselves. This is an important point to remember and an example for us to follow as Helps workers.

The notoriety, the praise, and the recognition are nothing; the privilege of serving Jesus Christ and its eternal rewards are what's important! The disciples knew that and conducted themselves accordingly. As you read the Bible, you will see that the people who wrote them down avoided personal aggrandizement and gave all the glory to God.

You will need to know a few terms to follow the instructions about faithfulness and commitment. We will look at Greek and Hebrew words and how we use these terms in the present day.

Pistos

Greek meaning faithful and steady. Questions 10–15 all used pistos to describe the actions and conduct of a person.

Other words for faith and faithfulness apply to faith in God, the faithfulness of God, etc. For example, in the Hebrew, faithfulness can be truthfulness. *Emun* is a faithful person or witness.

In this class, we do not downgrade these kinds of faith and faithfulness; rather, we pick out the scriptures on the topic of faithful workers.

Acts 6:3 requires your church leadership to determine that you are of honest report and wise and full of the Holy Spirit before you can be appointed to a position in the Helps Ministry. Faithfulness of the spiritual kind, Bible reading, and prayer are just important as faithfulness in a job or on-time activities. Both must show in your life to be judged as wise and full of the Holy Spirit. So let's go to the homework and give you a chance to share.

Faithfulness Scriptures

Numbers 12:7. Who was faithful in all things? **Moses.** He worked hard and took a lot of flak from his people while they were in the wilderness. He had to obey God's orders and did so faithfully. We expect Helps workers to be faithful to their calling too. Whatever you do, glorify God by your conduct and performance.

1 Samuel 2:35. Who is the faithful priest? *Jesus, the Messiah.* Jesus faithfully performed all that His Father told Him to do even to going to the cross. So when you are asked to make a sacrifice on occasion, remember the example of Jesus.

1 Samuel 22:14. Who was honorable in the Kings house? **David.** He went at the king's bidding; he knew who his boss was. Here again, we have an example of a man who did what he was told to do even in the face of criticism and jealousy. David learned what it was to follow even when it was tough so he could effectively lead others someday. When the going got tough for David and he had to require supreme effort from others, he could get it because others respected the way he lived his life and would follow his example.

Nehemiah 13:13. What do we call these people today? This was a hard one; you had to be creative and think of what this training is all about. The answer is **Helps Workers.** The lesson here is that their duties had to do with the public trust, money, and the distribution of valuable resources. Ushers, office staff, and audiovisual staff are all examples of workers who use or have charge of expensive equipment, money, or other resources of the church. All of us, however, must be trusted to do our jobs carefully, diligently, and skillfully to give glory to God.

Proverbs 14:5 This scripture tells us to tell the **truth** or be **people whose word is their bond.** Item 6 of the Code of Conduct speaks of being reliable and showing up when you sign up. You give your word when you sign something whether it be a loan document at a bank or the Code of Conduct here. The point is that we have to be examples to the church of truthfulness and reliability.

Proverbs 28:20. The faithful get *abundant blessings* while the money grubbers get *punished*. If all you are looking for in your life and in ministry is financial gain, you are in for some real sorrow. In 1 Timothy 6:10, we read of the love of money being the root of all evil. Run your finances in accordance with the Word of God. Remember that the promises of God all require some personal responsibility. God does not want you to be poor. Be faithful in your profession, your job, and your ministry. Let God bring the abundance as a result of your faithfulness in the tithe and in your work.

Isaiah 8:2. What did the faithful witnesses do? They *witnessed* and recorded it in *writing*. Why mention something this obvious? You won't always have the job. God may move you to another ministry, but He may not do that until you have written down what is necessary to do the job so the next person can do it with a minimum of instruction. Our denomination requires diligent record keeping of not just money but also property, salvations, baptisms, and other events. Our bylaws require some of these records to be accurately kept forever! Let's be good witnesses and record the results of our ministry.

Isaiah 25:1. What are God's Counsels of Old? *Faithfulness and truth.* This goes back again to the need to do something if we say we will do it. Our word must be our bond. Church membership for example: we say we will be members of this church and we join. *Emunah* is Hebrew for faithfulness or stability. Question number 6 makes the point that an emunah man will abound with blessings where the person who thinks only of riches is never innocent.

Jeremiah 23:28. Concerning speaking the Word. Your thoughts on this scripture. The Hebrew word here is *emeth*, "trustworthiness." In Jeremiah's time, God lost patience with priests and false prophets and spoke against them through Jeremiah. Our obligation is no less today; our church leaders and God must be able to trust us to speak and witness the Word of God, not our opinions or some compromise to appease people. We must live and speak the uncompromised Word of God.

(Instructor: have someone read Matthew 15:1–20.)

Jesus makes it very clear what He thinks of clergy who preach religion instead of the Word of God.

Matthew 24:45. Who was ruler over an entire household? *The faithful, or steady and wise servant.* The Greek word here is *pistos*. As you work in Helps, your leaders will observe you and how you perform your job. Promotion to greater responsibility will go to the faithful and wise servants. Acts 6:3 is the biblical instruction for your leadership. For those who aspire to full-time ministry, the practical skills learned in the Ministry of Helps can be a first step in ministry training and will prove invaluable to you later.

Experience has proven that as Helps workers learn the biblical truths about faithfulness and commitment, that spills over into their secular jobs and they see themselves prospering there. It may be why so many Sunday Christians separate their secular lives from being Christian and do it the world's way. They fail to realize that God's way is best for our Christian experience, our secular work, and recreation.

Matthew 25:21, 23. Why did the servants get rewarded? *Diligence in money matters*. Here again we have two faithful and wise servants and one who fell short. The two were publicly rewarded for their diligence; the one was chastised for slothfulness. As Helps workers, we expect that you will learn and appreciate God's laws of prosperity—seedtime and harvest, give and it will be given to you pressed down shaken together and running over. You will live a prosperous life. Look at Matthew 11:5; the poor will have the gospel preached to them. Jesus does not say the poor will be doing the preaching! Can we all agree that the good news to a poor person is, "You don't have to be poor anymore"? See also Joshua 1:8 and 3 John 2. Remember, as Helps workers, we are the example, so let's set a good one.

Ephesians 6:21. Tychicus was a *faithful minister in the Lord* sent by Paul to "make known to you all things, that you may know our affairs, and he might comfort you hearts." These few verses in the conclusion of the letter to the Ephesians speak volumes to us as workers sent out by our leaders. We must be faithful to the gospel and to our leadership to "know their affairs"—what they are teaching and preaching. Being a good minister and following a good minister are essential to the body of Christ. If seed is not sown, there cannot be a harvest. In our Christian walk, we may encounter believers who reject the Pentecostal/Charismatic movement. We cannot compromise our beliefs by agreeing with them, but we do not need to be disagreeable. Instead, we should find Christ and Him risen as the common place we can agree on and cheerfully agree to disagree on the charismatic gifts.

As Foursquare people, "We believe that the holy Bible is the Word of the living God—true, immutable, steadfast, and unchangeable, as its author the Lord Jehovah; that it was written by holy men of old as they were moved upon and inspired by the Holy Spirit." This is a portion of the first sentence of the Declaration of Faith written by Aimee Semple McPherson, the founder of Foursquare. The Word is our only guide, not religion.

1 Timothy 1:12. Jesus counted Paul *faithful* and put him **into the ministry**. Paul was a well-educated Jew who persecuted Christians. Before our salvation, many of us may have ridiculed people for "being holier than thou." They didn't smoke, drink, or cuss, and we felt uncomfortable. So God, through faith in Jesus Christ and the power of the Holy Spirit, gets us saved. Now it's our turn to be holy, hopefully not holier than thou, with attitude. Bur even being lovingly holy and pure in lifestyle will make others uncomfortable. We have to follow Paul's example. He quit killing Christians and sold out a hundred percent to Christ. We have no less a goal to attain. Let the world see that we are Christians by what we do and say in ministry and in our secular workplaces. We are ambassadors for Christ and need to be recognized as such without having to preach to anyone. If we aspire to the fivefold ministry, we should study to show ourselves approved, be faithful in word and deed, and let God do the calling and promoting.

2 Timothy 2:2. What must faithful men do here? *Teach others who are pistos—faithful—the Word.* Here, Timothy was admonished to teach other faithful people the things Paul taught him to others who could teach. We must do the same. This class and local Bible training centers do just that. They admit students who have been judged faithful (Acts 6:3—honest, full of the Holy Ghost and wisdom). We bring the gospel to everyone; we teach how to teach the gospel to faithful people. We do not throw our pearls before swine (Matthew 7:6).

When we share Jesus, let's do so with people who want to listen. If we try to cram the Word down someone's throat, we are wasting our time. We should give faithfully and lovingly with the unction of the Holy Spirit just the amount of Word they can handle at that time. Let us want to come back for more, not dread seeing us.

3 John 5. Doing *faithfully* whatever we can for the church and for others. The context here is a commendation to a man named Gaius for hospitality shown to the brethren and strangers. Gaius was a Helps worker of the highest order; 3 John is a very short book, and its theme is commending a person who like us works at tending to things in the church. Gaius was commended for his assistance to the ministers who traveled around in those days. Here is John, one if the inner circle of three with Jesus, a minister for perhaps fifty years at the time this book was written. He read a thank-you note to someone who helped and let him know he had done well. This message is to us, and in the same letter, we are told (along with Gaius) that God wishes us to be in good physical health and to prosper financially even as our souls (minds) prosper. I hope all Helps workers prosper and turn their minds to the Word of God with all the data that will make their Helps jobs go smoothly with things that will make them better persons, parents, children, and better employees or employers. I hope they take care of the temples of the Holy Spirit—their bodies that God has entrusted them with.

(Instructor: read the next few passages to get the participants ready for next week. It might be wise to remind them that the trouble they are going through to prepare themselves for ministry will be the same for all new workers. That way, everyone will have the same basic understanding of how things should be run and will cooperate with one another to do God's work in a loving and effective way.)

Before we go, will you share your remarks about the homework question of why do we need to be faithful if God will forgive us whether or not we are?

I hope this lesson on the forms of faithfulness and commitment will inspire you to be the person God wants you to be. Your pastor and the leadership of your church will give you the instruction and assistance necessary for you to become the pistos worker you desire to be. Please ask questions, seek out knowledge, make suggestions for improvement, and be an active participant in the living and breathing body of Christ.

Commit to God by becoming a member of this church; commit to your pastor and to the members of the church as Christ did. He died on the cross for you; all He asks for is your love and praise and faithfulness to His teachings.

Let me share an experience of a new pastor in town somewhere. It could have been anyone who was known to be a Christian. He was new in a small town, and he took a bus one day to avoid traffic and parking as he was unfamiliar with the area. When he got on the bus, he gave the driver a dollar and took his change to his seat. When he counted, he saw it was 25 cents too much. First, he said. "Praise God for the blessing! The bus company is big and can afford it." Then his conscience set in. He repented and gave the driver the quarter. The driver's response was, "I knew you were a new pastor (Christian) in town and decided to give you too much money back. If you gave it back, I was going to go to church. If you kept it, I would not." This pastor almost sold Jesus out for two bits! Others are watching us; others know we are Christians and are judging us and perhaps deciding whether to accept Jesus.

Let's be faithful to the teachings of God, stay in the Word, and do all that it written therein.

(Instructor: introduce the next three lessons.)

Our final three lessons have to do with church organization. We will see how Jesus was very organized. God is the master organizer; He spoke the world into existence in seven days and did not make one mistake!

We will learn about our denomination and our local church's organizational structure and take a short look at other forms of church governance in the United States and elsewhere today.

We will go over the academic part very quickly because we want to concentrate on how to start ministries in the church and get people thinking about how they fit into the local body. How can you help? We will discuss church discipline and organizational and staff relationships at the local level and in the denomination. Finally, we will go over how to start a ministry in the church.

Read ahead and write some questions in your notebooks.

(closing prayer)

LESSON 10

Church Governance

(Note to instructor: The next two lessons are ones that must be approached with the utmost sensitivity. Many American churchgoers, even leadership, have accused denominations and pastors of "laying bondage" on them! The media have not been kind to churches either. Thus, you may have folks attending your church who have had a bad experience with another church body or pastor. You even may have someone who has been in a cult where bondage was placed on them. We have a generation of churchgoers who grew up in the sixties and seventies and some later generations where kids learned to question authority. Many of them have a difficult time committing to any authority figure.

In America, we have a challenge to teach church government with gentleness and compassion. We must also be true to the Word and our denominational structure to clearly teach that the church is not a democracy. It was not in biblical times and is not today.

One thing is clear: those looking for the perfect church are in for a lifetime of frustration. You might remind folks that if they did find that perfect church, they might not be perfect enough to join!)

Materials needed

- Bible, one per student
- denominational organizational chart (usually available online)
- articles of incorporation and bylaws of your local church.

(Instructor: start instruction.)

The primary issues facing us as Christians in the twenty-first century are How do we operate our churches in a way that pleases God? How do we do it with a guidebook the last chapter of which was written 2,000 years ago? How do we do it in a way that complies with the secular government rules for "exempt status"?

Before we can get into the details of the structure, we must get one primary precept clear in our minds. Without understanding this, no serious study of church governance can be held.

The first concept is that Christianity is not a democracy. God is sovereign; His Word is truth. In Genesis, where He created everything by His Word., there was no interference by a deacon board or a vote by anyone. In the New Testament, He manifested Himself in the flesh as Jesus. Then even over the protestations of His elders (Matthew 16:22–23), there was never a vote or discussion. During Jesus's ministry on earth and afterward during the ministry of the apostles, we find no evidence to suggest that elders, deacons, or bishops ever had any control over the apostles or their appointed preachers. (what we call the fivefold ministry today). That is what the Bible teaches us, not our opinion or invention. We'll here about them shortly.

The second concept or precept that has to be understood is that all questions about church governance and operation are not answered in the Word of God. This sounds simple and obvious, but here is where many disagreements occur. For example, pulpit placement, decoration of churches, clergy apparel—all these things have had Christians at each other's throats each thinking the others are less Christian because of their stands on one or other of these issues. Let's be realistic and do it God's way. We are here to do the work Jesus began, not argue about things like this. The key is understanding the differences and then appreciating that there is a place in God's scheme of things for wat He has ordained and what He left for us to sort out. Once we have this separation clear in our minds, we can study church governance with a new freedom of understanding.

This is not small stuff; denominations have risen and fallen by majoring in the minors. Arguments over issues God is silent upon have created rules and laws in churches that God never intended. Even today, you can get thrown out of Jesus-believing churches for violating a denominational rule or tradition.

We do not judge churches for this; we merely point out that there are two sets of rules: God's and ours. We do not ignore our rules; rather, we must consider them in the context of God's Word. If they complement and uplift God's Word, they are okay.

God's Word admonishes us to obey those who have rule over us. Romans 13 is a good example of this. We will create rules necessary for order. If God's rules get first place in your church and you diligently read God's Word, as time passes, the flaky ecclesiastical law will just fall to the wayside from lack of attention. Do not criticize other denominations or churches or joke about their traditions. Concentrate on uplifting Jesus in your life and let them attend to theirs.

By joining a denomination, you pledge to follow the rules of that church, even those you're not happy about! That's all right; just realize that they are human rules and follow them. If you make a mistake, repent, ask for forgiveness, and carry on with life. Hebrews 13:17 exhorts us to obey those who rule over us. That includes our parents if we are children, our pastors and leaders, our bosses at work, and our denominations.

Ephesians 4:11–13 tells us that our preachers are gifts from God, so surely we can submit to them. In 1 Corinthians 1:10, we are admonished to speaking in one accord and obey the rules! Let's remember these basics as we study church governance.

Four Basic Types of Church Governance (back to our fill-ins)

Episcopal comes from the Greek *episcopos*, bishop or overseer. This is where the pastor has a bishop or overseer supervising him or her. The Catholic, Episcopal, and the International Church of the Foursquare Gospel share this type of government. (Foursquare is a modified form of this government.) Here, the local pastor has less control over what happens in the church as is evidenced in the Catholic and Episcopal denominations in which there is a liturgy from which they are not supposed to deviate during services.

Foursquare pastors are not told what to preach from the higher authorities (one of the modifications). Churches are usually not owned locally but by the denominations, and property cannot be purchased or sold except with the approval of the bishop or overseer (this is true in Foursquare too). In some cases, the local congregation might have some small say in the selection of its pastor, but the final decision is always with the bishop or overseer.

Presbyterian. Greek *presbuteros*, elder, and *presbuteroi*, the plural of the word. The words presbyter, bishop (Greek *episkopos*) and deacon (Greek *diakoneo*) were all common official titles used for leaders in society at that time. Since most people had one of these types of folks supervising them and they knew they had to follow the orders they gave, it was natural for the early church to adopt them as easy to understand words for leaders in the church. Obviously, they have stayed permanently in the church and have fallen out of use in secular society. In this form of governance, the presbyters (business leaders) of the church have the responsibility to operate the church and hire the pastor. Presbyterians use this method and others use variations of it.

Congregational. This third type has great favor in the United States. It is how we run our secular government and is very popular with a people who value freedom. Here, the congregation votes on major issues including hiring or firing a pastor, purchasing or selling property, who can be a member, and so on. Speculation is that this form of church governance prospered because so many of our citizens were immigrants from nations where the government controlled the church. Possibly, there was religious discrimination or suppression. It follows that when they got here, having a say in the church seemed to be a good thing to them. Today, great denominations such as the Assemblies of God, most of the Baptist denominations, and other denominations use this form of governance.

This form of governance is impossible to justify with the Word of God. There are no examples in the Old or New Testament of congregations starting churches or running them. All the examples are of the Levitical priesthood running the synagogues in the Old Testament and the apostles and their appointed leaders running the New Testament churches. The apostles appointed elders and leaders, not vice versa.

This does not make the congregational form of government or these churches bad, nor does it detract from the good they have done and continue to do. Sometimes, church politics gets in the way of what God is trying to do and takes people's minds off God and gets it on politics.

The challenge for people in these churches is being diligent in seeking God when they vote. Consider the candidates in the context of the Bible, not a popularity contest. Use Acts 6:3. Pretend you are an apostle and chose people who are honest, full of the Holy Spirit, and wise to appoint over your church.

The last form of government is the *Independent*. In this form of governance, the pastor or evangelist or other person in charge of the ministry is in fact the head of everything. Any elders, deacons or other advisors are chosen by that person and serve at his or her pleasure.

Examples of this form of governance are found in the ministry of Moses, who chose his own judges (with no vote) and Elijah, who chose his own successor (again without a vote or consultation with a board). All the Old Testament prophets and the New Testament apostles followed God's direction for their lives and ministries and were led by the Holy Spirit, not a board of deacons.

If we examine the organization of Jesus's ministry, we find the same pattern. Jesus ran the show and appointed those of His choosing to positions of authority. In the Old Testament days, we frequently read examples of those who did not like what one or another of the prophets said (or even what Jesus said). The prophets still stayed the prophets; no one fired them. Today, many independent churches function this way.

Many pastors do not have a business background and rely heavily on their church elders for advice. In the Congregational and Presbyterian forms of governance, the pastor may be obligated to take the advice of the elders. In the Episcopal and Independent forms, they may take it or not as they wish.

God has given us free will and wants us to praise and honor Him. One of the ways we honor God is by honoring His gifts to us—our pastors and others in ministry. While we may feel more comfortable having control over our pastor with the vote, this has nothing to do with God's way of doing business. Some churches even have pulpit committees to suggest to the pastor what should be preached!

In 1 Timothy 6:20–21, Paul gave Timothy an admonition; grant me the privilege of embellishing it: "O Timothy, keep (observe) God's Word and keep (observe) his congregation which is committed to your trust. Avoid profane babbling and contradictions of what is called knowledge (like arguments with the church boards and elders) especially when those profess scientific knowledge superior to the pastor and which strays from the faith."

(Instructor: ask for examples from the class.)

Let's do a brief recap before we proceed to specific governance practices of this church. What are the two precepts we must keep in mind? (Ask the class.)

- First, Christianity is not a democracy.
- Second, all things concerning operation of a church are not answered in the Bible.

The four general forms of church government

- Episcopal
- Presbyterian
- Congregational
- Independent

The name of our church is (your official church name here)
What are some of the things we need to do to get organized so people who come from one

church in our denomination to another can expect the same statements of faith and standards of worship? What follows is a suggested list. Your list should be verbatim from your major denomination or group of churches. For example,

- Organize a structure that can govern a large, multinational organization.
- License and ordain clergy so there is a standard known to all.
- Establish churches or grant charters to established churches that wish to join us.
- Establish, own, and operate educational institutions of collegiate and less than collegiate grade.
- Establish, maintain, and conduct missionary endeavors for the furtherance of the gospel in the United States and the world.
- Do other things needed to further the gospel.

The primary focus of the pastor is outlined in Ephesians 4:11–16. Additionally, pastors are encouraged to multiply themselves (see Acts 6:3) choosing from among their congregation honest people full of the Holy Spirit and wisdom to do the work of the church. That is what this class is all about—a place where the pastor and leadership can observe you and judge your wisdom, honesty, and evidence of the Holy Spirit in your life. Also through the encouragement of members to attend Bible colleges or even starting one in their church.

(Instructor: lessons 10 and 11 may overlap. If you did not finish this lesson, make it up next time and shorten the next lesson.)

LESSON 11

Discipline and Organizational and Staff Relationships in the Local Body

This is a continuation of the last lesson. We now move to the local level. Pastors typically appoint support people to one-year terms to assist in the ministry to the local congregation. In some cases, they are elected each year. Either way, the person in that office must have completed Helps Ministry training or they would be ineligible to serve.

(You may have to amend your bylaws to make this effective.)

Some of those offices are

(You may have to do extensive rewriting of this chapter to correctly state the organizational relationships created by your church bylaws, denominational structure, and possibly local preference for names of positions.)

Associate Pastor. One who is related in function to the senior pastor, the second overseer of the entire congregation. This position takes the broad view of the congregation and church as a body.

Assistant Pastors. These ministers are more specialized. They may oversee a function or a group of functions such as music, children's pastor, youth pastor, administrators, minister of visitation, and other are assistants. They are licensed and ordained clergy serving a pastor and must resign when that pastor leaves, thus leaving the new pastor with the freedom to appoint leaders he or she selects (Acts 6:3).

Pastors also hire clerical, administrative, and maintenance people to run the secular operations necessary at a church. These jobs are generally filled by regular church members, but they are not licensed or ordained, and they do not have to resign their jobs when there is a change of pastor.

The pastor usually has the ultimate responsibility for all functions in a church; all performing jobs in those various functions must subordinate themselves to the pastor. The person in that ministerial office has to take the heat if people mess up, so he or she has to have the authority and power to supervise them. This is usually done by creating an organizational chart and delegating responsibility and authority to assistants and leaders in various functions.

For example, when the leader of the audiovisual department gives direction to one of the workers in that department, it is the same as if the pastor had given that direction. Following that instruction is not subject to debate or argument; the audiovisual person just does it.

We do things we don't really enjoy on our jobs, and some parts of every job are tedious, but someone has to do it. Likewise in the church, a leader may ask you to do something you aren't thrilled about. Show your love of God by doing the task without comment particularly during a service.

Maintain and respect the organizational structure. Let supervisors supervise; refrain from jumping in and correcting a worker who is assigned to another leader. Tell the leader privately, and let the leader handle the training or discipline. Unless there is danger to someone, do not interfere with another person's job. As leaders, we must be instant in season to assist anywhere we are needed including cleaning toilets if that's necessary. Jesus washed feet, so we can clean toilets. We must demonstrate to the congregation that we are servants, not bosses. We cannot be perceived as being too good to do something.

Matthew 18:15 gives specific instructions about how disagreements are to be handled. In the Helps Ministry, the witnesses you choose should be other members of your ministry group who agree with you. "Taking it to the church" is not telling your story to everyone in the congregation; it's going up another level to the immediate supervisor of your supervisor. You go to the pastor only if that person is your supervisor's supervisor. Differences of opinion between workers should not be discussed with spouses, children, or others who might spread gossip. Let's resolve disagreements in the Helps Ministry, not bring disputes into the congregation.

- 1 Peter 8:3–13 is the Bible for the above: let's be in one accord, speaking well of one another, not speaking evil of anyone. Peter is speaking to us here.
- Hebrews 13:17 admonishes us to obey those who have rule over us.

Elsewhere in the Word, we are told to "esteem our leaders highly in love." Let's see how God wants us to feel love and esteem. *Beseech* in this context is stronger than asking as a child would a parent; it is not an order but an asking from a equal to an equal. Here we have Paul beseeching us!

Talking to us as equal to equal, let's read 1 Thessalonians 5:12–13, in which Peter is writing to pastors and spiritual leaders. He uses the term *elder*; in this context, the Greek is *sumpresbuteros*, fellow elder, not just plain *presbuteros*, which is an elder. He uses the familiar "fellow elder"; imagine a fellow elder with a guy like Peter, the man from the inner circle with Jesus Himself! (not just your plain old elder). We read in 1 Peter 5:1–4,

> The elders who are among you I exhort, I who am a fellow elder and a witness of the sufferings of Christ, and also a partaker of the glory that will be revealed: 2 Shepherd the flock of God which is among you, serving as overseers, not by compulsion but willingly, not for dishonest gain but eagerly; 3 nor as being lords over those entrusted to you, but being examples to the flock; 4 and when the Chief Shepherd appears, you will receive the crown of glory that does not fade away.

For an example of organization, look at what Jesus accomplished in three years.

- He ran His ministry and did not back off from any challenge. He was fearless. We must be the same even in the face of adversity.

- He appointed three assistant or associate pastors to help Him—Peter, James, and John. Pastors or church leadership should be doing this to train the next generation.

- He had a leadership team of the twelve (including the senior staff). Most churches have a church board and leaders in specific ministries.

- He had a cadre of helpers, the seventy He trained and sent out. He later recharged them (Luke 10:1–20). This class was the first of many to equip you for future ministry.

- He set the example of multiplication to spread the Word further and faster. The apostles (except Judas Iscariot) all went out and preached, taught, and started churches. They also raised up new preachers who did the same; we are the result of that process.

How about an oral snap quiz? I'll ask the question and everyone can say the answer.

1. God's kingdom is not a democracy—true or false?
2. The four forms of church government in the order studied.

   - Episcopal
   - Presbyterian
   - Congregational
   - Independent

3. Our church is an example of (place your church in one of the classes or combination of classes).
4. The highest authority in our church or denomination is (name that office here).

Next week is our final class. It is a big deal, and it is very important for everyone to read ahead and completely understand next week's lesson whether you are an usher or not. The lesson is intended to acquaint you with the process of creating a ministry outline that can be the basis of any ministry. We are using the outline for the ushering ministry as our example. Thus, you learn about ushering in case we have to draft you on occasion, and using that outline, you will learn about how to write and plan an outline for another ministry all in one lesson.

Those of you in ministries other than ushering should write down some ideas for a ministry you are interested in that we can discuss next week. That way, all the class can participate in really sketching out a new ministry outline using this example. Please do the homework

(closing prayer)

LESSON 12

How to Start a Ministry in the Church

We are at the end of our twelve-week Adventure in Practical or Helps Ministry. I hope you all have enjoyed it.

(Instructor: Someone once said that if the class says no, then leave; this lesson will never bail you out!)

We will use the ushering ministry as our example; we will learn how to write a ministry outline. I hope you have read ahead and have gone over these pages. We will start with questions and find out your thoughts on two things. First, consider the ushering ministry as outlined in this lesson and compare how we do this job today with that model. How does it compare with the model? Can we or should we make improvements? What does the class think?

Second, has anyone begun his or her ministry outline for some other ministry using this as a model? If not, does anyone have an idea for a new ministry? Can we discuss its organization using what we learned by reading ahead in this lesson?

> Proverbs 24:3–4: "A house is built by wisdom, and is set up by understanding. By discretion the chambers are filled with all precious and excellent wealth."

Three key words: *wisdom*, *knowledge* (understanding), and *common sense* (discretion). Let's look at some places we've seen these words before. Turn to Acts 6:3. Do we remember how workers are chosen? Wasn't wisdom one of them?

Let's remember 3 John 2; as you recall, this was written to Gaius, our bigtime example of a successful and faithful Helps worker. Remember our souls are the mind, emotions, and intellect.

When we develop a ministry outline, we want to use all the tools God gave us. His Word guides us spiritually, and in all functions, we see these three thoughts or words wisdom, knowledge, and common sense. These concepts must guide us in our actions; they are the principal factors that cover the technical (nonbiblical) side of the ministry.

There is also a sneaky reason for using the ushering ministry.

- First, ushering is present in all churches and all denominations. So all of us have observed an usher and have an idea of what normally goes on. And it follows that it will be easier to use this as our example since it is familiar. In some churches, the duties may be minimal—in others, very complex. So our outline will be very thorough and detailed, perhaps more detailed than needed. This is for instructional purposes.

- Second, the pastor and the head usher gets the bonus of having 100 percent of their Helps workers qualified to usher if the need arises. If an emergency substitute is needed, there is a minimum of training needed.

You may never have to put together a ministry, but you may have to assist whomever is doing it with some of the details, so listen carefully and make a lot of notes on how you would do it if you were in charge. You might be some day!

There is a lot of room in your manuals for you to jot down notes for a ministry you might want to start. The workbooks are yours; mark them up all you want.

Format: Everything in italics in your copy of this chapter is instruction about the ministry outline. What is written in regular type is the ministry outline.

The first thing is to write a paragraph or so to let people know what is in the job description. And, I might add, let them know the attitude needed for success.

Job Description for Ushering Ministry

First paragraph: Ushers are the most visible of workers during a service. They may take the offering, seat people, serve communion, and are generally more visible to the congregation. Thus, they must represent God, the pastor, and the leadership of the church in an honorable way.

The best ushers are like waiters at a fancy restaurant. They seem to get everything done almost before you ask for it, and they do it in a way that you don't notice how hard they are working. In the church, Jesus gets the glory, and the pastor or other in the pulpit get the attention, not the ushers. Here is a quick overview. Some jobs, seating, offering etc. Something about attitude and honor. And an example everyone can relate to. And something about not being the center of attention.

The second paragraph: The guidelines in this job description will assist you in performing outstanding service to God and the local body. They are not laws to be obeyed; they are a structure we use to ensure everyone is in one accord. According to Acts 2:1, if we are to expect baptisms in the Holy Spirit and other manifestations of the Spirit in our church, we must be in one accord. Also, instructions reduce the need for decision making, and things run smoother.

The third paragraph introduces the job description and gives biblical basis for being organized and "in one accord."

Many duties are required—turning on lights, adjusting heat, inspecting bathrooms, etc. Others require the leading of the Holy Spirit and suppose that the usher is operating supernaturally on the job. An example would be someone throwing a noisy fit during the sermon. When do you remove them? What do you say to them? Where do you take them? You won't find the answers written here. The Holy Spirit must take charge then. Your pastor or other in the pulpit may have the unction of the Holy Spirit and give direction. But you will do the work and you will say the words. So be prayed up, operate in love, and maintain an attitude of a servant, not an enforcer of the rules (Philippians 2:2–4).

(Instructor: That final paragraph suggests some of the duties and starts the reader thinking, *How do I do this? Maybe I do need some training.* And finally, another biblical basis for how to operate in the ministry.)

Remember, some have never read a job description either at their workplaces or in a church. Make it simple but complete so everyone knows the definition of a job well done. The introduction should just be enough to give a little overview but not get into a lot of detail about the job performance.

Job Duties

These are examples. You must tailor your job description to your church and cover only what the usher does. In a small church, they may do almost everything; in a larger church, they will be more specialized and even have numbered positions.

- Ushers should arrive early; head usher ten minutes before the others.
- They should make sure the church is clean and tidy including bathrooms.
- Chairs set up correctly
- Parking lot, entry, and sidewalks policed
- A/C or heat properly adjusted
- Proper doors unlocked (or locked)

(The above items may be handled by janitorial staff or ministry if you have one. In small churches, the users do it.)

- Overhead projector readied unless you have an audiovisual ministry
- Offering containers positioned for use with envelopes and visitor information close at hand.
- Water and cups placed for pulpit and musicians. Tissues and anointing oil at or near the altar.
- Covers or drop cloths available for female altar attendants/ushers.
- Dress and grooming to the standard of the church. Some may have badges or special coats for ushers so they can be identified.

Here, let's remember other ministries that may have special dress needs. Women in the nursery or with little children must wear pants, not dresses or skirts. They may have to assume unflattering positions to ride herd on the kids, and we do not want any embarrassment.

Clean shaven or neat beards. Take a vacation from your duties while you cultivate your beard.

Clean of body and breath. Have breath mints handy, and use deodorant.

If you have the sniffles or other attacks of the enemy that might offend or be contagious, call your supervisor and do not serve that week. This is especially important when working with children

As you add to your list, let your imagination run wild. The first copy is for you alone anyway, so put everything you can conjure up down on paper. Remember that you may have a new person to church who knows nothing about the technicalities of working in your ministry. You can always edit; just don't forget anything important.

Know where all church facilities are. Little maps can be duplicated so each usher has one. When someone asks directions of an usher, it is not a good thing to reply, "I don't know."

Following the above, provide a list of all church leaders. The council, pastors and key leaders should listed with their contact information (with their permission) and given to each usher so he or she can point to the correct person when asked and so you can advise the correct person when a ministry opportunity turns up in his or her area.

Make an effort to seat folks in the front seats first so the latecomers do not disrupt the service. (Some churches block off the last two rows until the song service is half over.)

Opening Prayer

Sometime prior to the start of their duties, the head usher should gather the workers and perhaps the music people and pray for the pastor and for needs to be met during the service. Then, while you are at your position, intercede in the Spirit when you are not actually performing a task.

Ushers should pray quietly in tongues while standing behind someone in a prayer line (catching).

Maintain decency and order in love. During the gifts of the Spirit, prohibit entry and movement in the service as best you can without being too obvious.

Pray for crying children, inattentive teens, and full bladders so distractions due to noise and movement are minimized.

Be ready at all times to cast out demons, to lay hands on the sick so they may be healed, and for salvation and baptism in the Holy Spirit.

Work inconspicuously; people are supposed to have their attention on the giving of the Word, not the workers.

Future leaders take note: some enter Helps to be noticed; they my see this as their opportunity to become somebody. But the best church workers do it as worship to the Lord, not as a way to aggrandize themselves. Be aware; if you see the tendency to "Look at me!" nip it in the bud.

The head usher is usually in charge of the sanctuary when the pastor is in the pulpit. Emergency messages, needs, or gifts of the Holy Spirit for the edification of the church should be presented to the head usher. Don't just let people walk up to the platform (unless that is the preference of the pastor).

The pastor and head usher should have prearranged signals for use during the service.

During services, the head usher leads all ministries and can direct the activities of any worker. Before and after service, the normal organizational table applies. Head ushers must be sensitive to the other leaders and let them lead their people whenever possible.

Sometimes, ushers will be separated from their families during a service. Rotate them so it happens as little as possible. When you are with family, do not hold babies; you must be able to act immediately.

Keep your eyes open even when the pastor says, "All eyes closed." You must be able to spot people fidgeting or raising their hands slightly and point them out to the exhorters or a pastor later. Also, you must guard the assembly from someone who would disrupt during an altar call. You can "get into the Spirit" when you are not needed on your job. That is what rotation is all about.

As leaders, we must adequately staff each ministry so there is backup and extras so no one burns out. It is better to go without a ministry than to do it with an inadequate number of people and have it fall apart because everyone gets used too much. This is part of the planning process. How many do you need? Are there enough willing people to fill the need on an ongoing basis?

Offerings

Take your cue from the person in the pulpit. They may want the ushers to clap and stomp in joy at the mention of an offering, or they may want it more dignified. Some pass the bucket or plate; others bring it up front. This is local option, but it needs to be clear to both ushers and congregation.

Counting the Offering

Always have two people count, and rotate the people so the same two do not always serve together. This prevents ushers from getting too familiar with who is giving and who is not. Also, switching pairs reduces the possibility that the tempter can enter into the process and steal. The head usher should rotate through this detail along with the other ushers and church leaders.

Any time you have a ministry with valuable property or money, you must have adequate safeguards in place. We are stewards of God's property and we must take it seriously.

Assisting with Communion

A set procedure must be developed—who comes in early and sets up, who cleans up, and which usher does the platform, the audiovisual, and the children's church. Lay it out item by item so there is a clear picture of who does what. Confusion must not occur during a service.

Altar Calls

This is a specialized part of ushering that is not done everywhere. In major ministries and many prominent evangelists' ministries, we see large altar calls with many users acting as directors and "catchers." In the local church, this happens less often. However, wise planning suggests that having a written plan in effect and training in operating during an altar call is essential if it is to go smoothly.

Some additional tips and suggestions for your outline: When you have guest ministers, the head usher should talk with them and get their preferences. If they have none, explain your usual method of operation and get their agreement not to change things in the middle of the service.

Keep lines in order; lines should be only one person deep so catchers can move freely behind them. People waiting should be kept in the aisles and "fed" up front as space permits.

Let no one touch the person being prayed for except the minister in charge. He or she will ask for help if necessary. Just pray in tongues (quietly) behind them and watch (and listen to) the preacher and the person you are behind.

Catchers should hold at the elbow and small of the back, not the armpits. Armpit catching can ruin your back and your reputation if your hands go around the front of a female.

A female usher should always be present and instantly place a drop cloth over females preferably on the way down. This takes grace and finesse, but with practice, it is easily done.

Have ushers in the rear to control movement and noise.

Unless the service has been dismissed from the pulpit, folks should be encouraged to stay in their seats and pray.

Again, ushers do not close their eyes and bow their heads during altar calls unless they are in the front seats; they bow but keep their eyes open. They have to be able to identify timid folks who fidget or partially raise their hands and have someone lovingly ask if they need prayer. Ushers point them out to the exhorters or prayer team for follow-up.

Ushers positions should be numbered, and separate job outlines should be written for each position. Number 1 is the primary catcher and sits up front; number 2 sits on the other side in the front. They are responsible for keeping order on the platform and are the primary catchers. Female ushers or other designated females should also be in front for covering duties.

Ushers number 3, 4, and higher numbers are farther back in the sanctuary.

The head usher will usually stay in the back until the altar call and then move to the front to direct people into the prayer line and supervise the ushers in front. The head usher will also read signals from the pastor or pulpit minister and advise the prayer team about the need of the person is so after the altar call they can follow up and give encouragement or a tract or a Bible if it is a salvation.

Outside/parking lot duties are where ushers rotate so they can be with their families during service. Outside ushers have no duties during service, so they are free to "get in the spirit," participate fully in worship, and not be bothered about any duties.

There must be depth in ministry; we cannot have the same people doing the same thing all the time. This can cause people to feel used. Also they cannot be ministered to if they are always ministering.

Because it is for training, this outline is purposely very detailed. In your outline, you need to cover what has to be done, who will be doing it, and how they should do it.

Giving workers an outline lets them know the definition of a good job and gives them something to aspire to. Some might fear that the job is too complicated or that they have no experience. Explain that you have outlines and will give training. Once they believe they can do it, they can.

When you make your list of things, arrange it in order of what has to be done down to what would be nice to have done. List the things that are inflexible such as being saved and baptized in the Holy Spirit, being on time, showing up when you promise to first, then go down in importance to the preference items.

To Review

- first, the title page with the two- or three-paragraph description of the ministry and what it accomplishes
- next, the list of the duties with the mandatory first down to the preference items
- in some ministries, there may be monetary considerations. The leader must address this issue separately, not in the job description, but the subject must be addressed so the leadership can make judgments on whether there are sufficient resources considering other needs of the church.

(Instructor: closing remarks.)

We have appreciated your attendance at these classes. If you have questions or comments, please feel free to make them. This series of classes is constantly being upgraded, and we earnestly solicit your input. Your pastor will present your certificate of completion at a church service soon. God bless you all, and may God get all the glory for the good work you do.

(closing prayer)

Printed in the United States
By Bookmasters